# MYTHIC TROY

# MYTHIC TROY

## The Complete Story
### Legend, Archaeology, and Intuition

Kevin J. Todeschi

ARE
PRESS

ASSOCIATION FOR
RESEARCH AND
ENLIGHTENMENT

A.R.E. Press • Virginia Beach • Virginia

A.R.E. Press
215 67th Street
Virginia Beach, VA 23451-2061

Library of Congress Cataloguing-in-Publication Data
Todeschi, Kevin J.
    Mythic Troy : the complete story : legend, archaeology, and intuition
/ by Kevin J. Todeschi.
        p.    cm.
    Includes bibliographical references and index.
    ISBN 0-87604-493-3 (trade pbk.)
    1. Mthology, Greek.  2. Trojan war.  I. Title.
BL783.T63 2004
398.2'0938—dc22

                                    2004007285

Cover design by Richard Boyle

*For Tyler Michael*

Once every people in the world believed that trees were divine, and could take human or grotesque shape and dance among the shadows; and that deer, and ravens and foxes, and wolves and bears, and clouds and pools, almost all things under the sun and moon, and the sun and moon, were no less divine and changeable.

They saw in the rainbow the still bent bow of a god thrown down in negligence; they heard in the thunder the sound of his beaten water-jar, or the tumult of his chariot wheels; and when a sudden flight of wild ducks, or of crows passed over their heads, they thought they were gazing at the dead hastening to their rest; while they dreamed of so great a mystery in little things that they believed the waving of a hand, or of a sacred bough, enough to trouble far-off hearts, or hood the moon with darkness.

W.B. Yeats

# Contents

# INTRODUCTION

The word "myth" is a derivative of the Greek word "mythos" and generally refers to a story or a legend. A myth can be based entirely on fantasy or it may have its origin in fact. In the ancient world, long before there was a written tradition, storytellers and poets passed on both history and legend orally from one generation to another. In addition to the possibility of containing accurate historical information, these myths often included universal or archetypal patterns of human experience and emotion that educated and inspired the listener. Even today these mythic tales can arouse something deep within the human psyche, often capturing the imagination of countless people, generations, and even entire cultures and continents.

For a time, mythic tales in the form of epic poems were passed along orally in exchange for food, accommodations, or sometimes money. These tales often embodied the stories of heroes and portrayed incredible achievement in the face of tremendous odds. They included accounts of human tragedy and unbelievable suffering, designed to show an audience that they were not alone in possessing hopes and dreams or in having to experience personal loss and pain. These epic tales often celebrated history, religion, and human virtues, as well as the many frailties of the mortal condition. They sometimes provided the listener with models of right and wrong conduct and with characters that exemplified supreme values and ideal behavior. In some instances, they attempted to examine the relationship between that which was human and that which was divine by presenting the interactions between mortals and the gods.

One of the greatest mythic tales of the ancient world is the epic of the Trojan War. It is the story of Paris, the young and perhaps foolish prince of Troy, who sought Helen, the most beautiful woman in the world, to be his own. Unfortunately, she was already the wife of another man: Menelaus, one of the Grecian kings. According to legend, that action prompted a ten-year war between Greece and Troy and led to the eventual annihilation of the Trojan civilization. In the tale, the two sides each experience their share of victory and defeat, luck and misfortune, and pain and rejoicing. The Greek hero Achilles becomes most prominent among all of the Greek forces while his Trojan counterpart, Hector, who was the brother of Paris, becomes the most outstanding warrior among his people. The myth of the Trojan War, the unrivaled beauty of Helen, the intrigue of the Trojan horse, and the heroism of warriors on both sides of the conflict have inspired and amazed countless individuals for thousands of years. Legend even claims that Alexander the Great (356–323 B.C.) took the story with him into battle for inspiration on his own military campaigns (Rieu, page vii).

Rather than existing only from a single source, the story of the Trojan War was well known among the Greeks, as it was handed down for hundreds of years from one generation to another. To be sure, the most famous account of the Trojan War is contained in Homer's *Iliad*, but it is generally believed that Homer did not create the story of the Trojan War; rather he based his epic on legends and stories that already existed during his time. In fact, the earliest known representation of the Trojan horse exists on an eighth-century B.C. vase, found on Mykonos, suggesting that the story of the horse was known even before the creation of Homer's epic poems (Wood, pg. 80). In Homer's account of the Trojan conflict, the war is between Troy and the various city-states of the Achaeans[1], ancestors to the ancient Greeks.

In the ancient world, it was the method of epic poets to take pieces of historical information and construct their own tales of fancy for the amusement and education of their audiences. By most accounts, Homer lived ca. 750–700 B.C., whereas the events of the Trojan War are generally dated nearly five hundred years earlier to around 1200 B.C. In fact, legend has it that the actual date of the fall of Troy occurred in 1184 B.C. Rather than detailing the conflict, the story of the *Iliad* essentially covers a fifty-day period in the tenth year of the Trojan War. In fact, most epics traditionally begin in the middle of the action, which in Latin is referred to as *in medias res* ("in the middle of things"). Homer's tale often refers to that which has gone before and hints at that which will come after—events that would have all been familiar to the Greeks. Homer's other celebrated volume, the *Odyssey*, explores the adventures of the Greek hero Odysseus (known as Ulysses in Latin) following the events of the Trojan War. Whereas the *Iliad* is generally considered a tragedy, the *Odyssey* presents a more romanticized view of life.

In spite of Homer's fame as the author of two of the greatest classics of all time, little is known about the poet himself. In fact, because there is no concrete evidence to prove otherwise, throughout history many scholars have questioned the literal existence of a single poet named "Homer." Some scholars have even suggested that the *Iliad* was composed by a variety of poets who each added their own creativity and style to an epic that changed and grew with the passage of time. Others contend that Homer did exist and was not only the single author of the

---

[1]For simplicity, throughout this volume the Achaeans will simply be referred to as the Greeks.

*Iliad* but of the *Odyssey*, as well (Rieu, xi). Because of the dialect he used in his poems, those who subscribe to the literal existence of Homer believe that he lived somewhere near the west coast of Asia Minor. One legend even suggests that Homer was a blind minstrel who traveled the coast, singing and reciting his epics, and that the portrayal of the blind minstrel Demodocus in the *Odyssey* may be, in part, a biographical sketch of the poet himself. Most scholars, however, doubt the validity of this claim.

In the first century B.C., approximately seven hundred years after Homer, the Italian poet Virgil (70–19 B.C.) took some of the characters and events in Homer's epic and created a new epic, called the *Aeneid*, that became a classic in its own right. Rather than being an oral work, the *Aeneid* was a written poem and followed the post-war adventures of the Trojan hero Aeneas and a small remnant of the Trojan civilization on their journey to the shores of a new country. Legend has it that their descendants would eventually found and establish the Roman Empire.

The *Aeneid* is considered the greatest classic of ancient Rome and was based in style on Homer's *Iliad* and *Odyssey*. The book was written at the request of the Roman emperor Augustus, who was a personal friend of the author. In terms of the Trojan War, only the second book relates to the fall of Troy; the rest of the book deals with the adventures of the surviving Trojans, led by Aeneas. The purpose of the epic was to essentially detail how the Roman Empire and its people traced itself to the survivors of Troy. Although other works and fragments of works exist and discuss various aspects of the Trojan myth, taken together the works of Homer and Virgil are certainly the most well-known accounts of the Trojan War and are often considered the greatest poems of antiquity.

In addition to the lives of the characters Achilles, Hector, Helen, and Paris, perhaps the most celebrated element of the Trojan myth is the story of the Trojan horse. Contrary to popular belief, however, the *Iliad* does not mention the Trojan horse. Homer's *Iliad* actually ends with the death of Hector, even before the destruction of Troy. Discussion of the fall of Troy and the Greeks' deception through the use of the Trojan horse is briefly mentioned in Homer's *Odyssey* and to a greater extent in Virgil's *Aeneid*.

In spite of the notoriety of the Trojan myth, for hundreds of years the characters from the Trojan War and even the city of Troy itself were regarded by much of history as legendary with no basis in fact. That view changed completely, however, in 1870 when German-born, American citizen and amateur archaeologist Heinrich Schliemann (1822-1890) began excavating an ancient city in Turkey not too far distant from the Aegean Sea and the Dardanelle strait (an important ancient link in the waterway connecting the Mediterranean Sea with the Black Sea). In time, further excavations would suggest that Troy had truly existed and had been destroyed by fire around the twelfth century B.C., at a time corresponding with Homer's legendary account.

Unfortunately, rather than solving the legitimacy of Troy once and for all, Schliemann's life and work seemed instead to add even greater mystery to the tale. A self-made millionaire, Schliemann became known not only for his discovery but also, critics often suggest, for his emotional coldness, his love of wealth, his frequent self-promotion, and his propensity to lie, break the law, or even destroy archaeological ruins in pursuit of his own interests. Even Schliemann's claims of having had a lifelong interest in finding Troy and of numbering among his possessions such treasures as the ashes of the Greek hero Odysseus and the crown jewels of the Trojan Empire have been disputed since his death. There is also some question as to whether or not Schliemann should receive full credit for having discovered Troy when it appears as if his work may have simply continued that begun by others. However, what cannot be disputed is that after Schliemann the story of Troy's existence, which had once been regarded as mythic history, suddenly appeared to become historical fact.

Fifty years after Schliemann's discovery, Edgar Cayce (1877-1945), a most unlikely source in Virginia Beach, Virginia, would reveal further insights into the story of Troy that added additional credence to the historical validity of the tale. Called "the most documented psychic of all time," Cayce for years had been providing individuals with intuitive glimpses into history, often providing information not known by contemporary society. In addition to speaking of the civilizations of ancient Egypt, ancient Persia, Palestine at the time of Jesus, and even the fabled continent of Atlantis, Cayce gave psychic readings to a number of individuals who, he claimed, were personally connected to the story of Troy.

Regardless of how unusual Edgar Cayce's talent for retrocognition—the ability to see clairvoyantly into the past—might sound, it has been repeatedly demonstrated that many of Cayce's historical insights have been accurate. Rather than being the stuff of fantasy, much of his psychic data has been confirmed by science and history. In fact, oftentimes information Cayce provided that may have appeared preposterous or seemed to contradict accepted scientific opinion at the time has later been validated. Examples include his statement that ancestors of human beings had been upon the earth generally and in North America specifically for thousands of years longer than science claimed in the 1930s and 1940s. On other occasions, he discussed how the Nile once flowed westward and emptied into the Atlantic Ocean, which was confirmed more than fifty years later by imaging radar technology aboard the U.S. space shuttle in the 1980s.[2] Another example is that the Cayce information frequently spoke about the existence of a Jewish sect called the Essenes that was made up of both male and female initiates who had once been part of a thriving community. It wasn't until after Cayce's death that the discovery of the Dead Sea scrolls and the existence of a community at Qumran came to public awareness.[3]

Edgar Cayce's psychic exploration of Troy was based in part upon the soul history of Cayce himself. A Christian mystic, Cayce became interested in the topic of reincarnation because of his own psychic information. After examining the biblical basis for reincarnation and seeing how clearly it connected an individual's experiences and actions from the past with her or his choices and probabilities in the present, he came to accept the concept.

---

[2]According to *Science* magazine (August 1986) imaging radar from the U.S. space shuttle discovered previously unknown river valleys beneath the Sahara suggesting that the present-day Nile had changed its course, once flowing across the African continent and emptying into the Atlantic Ocean. A directional change that Cayce had cited once in 1931 (276-2) and twice in 1932 (364-13 and 5748-6).

[3]A further examination of Cayce's life and work can be found in Sidney D. Kirkpatrick's *Edgar Cayce: An American Prophet* (2001).

The first mention of Troy in the Cayce material came on November 7, 1923. On that date Cayce gave a psychic reading to inquire about the past-life connections between himself and three individuals that were interested in financing Cayce's psychic work. Those individuals included Arthur Lammers, a printer and advertiser from Ohio; Linden Shroyer, an accountant and personal secretary to Lammers; and George Klingensmith, a construction engineer. During the course of the reading, Cayce mentioned that they had been together during the Trojan War essentially as warriors and guards (5717-5[4]). According to notes on file in the Edgar Cayce archives, after that date Cayce repeatedly told his longtime secretary, Gladys Davis, that he had once been associated with each of these three individuals for "destructive purposes." For that reason, Cayce surmised, they had come together in the present in the hope that they would somehow learn to work constructively together.

Follow-up questions about Edgar Cayce's Trojan experience were not asked until February 1924 when Cayce obtained a life reading for himself about his entire soul history. That reading stated that he had once lived in the city of Troy as an individual named Xenon. According to the information, Xenon had experienced a varied life as a student, a chemist, a sculptor, and an artist and eventually as a reluctant soldier, conscripted into the service of Troy with the onslaught of the Greek-Trojan conflict (294-8). Because of the cyclic nature of reincarnation and the fact that individuals pick up relationships where they have been left off, in addition to the three individuals who had already been cited, others who had been involved with him during that period would also reappear, the reading went on to suggest. One year later a twenty-nine-year-old Jewish stockbroker, who would have a tremendous impact upon the Cayce work, received his own life reading and was told that he had been none other than the fabled Greek nemesis of Troy, Achilles (900-38).

---

[4]During Cayce's life, the Edgar Cayce readings were all numbered to provide confidentiality. The first set of numbers (e.g., "5717") refers to the individual or group for whom the reading was given. The second set of numbers (e.g., "5") refers to the number in the series from which the reading is taken. For example, 5717-5 identifies the reading as the fifth one given to the individual assigned #5717.

Because of his own life experiences, challenges, and the various demands on his time, it was not until 1935 that Edgar Cayce explored his lifetime as Xenon in further detail. During a follow-up reading, Cayce learned that he had "lost" in terms of soul development in his Trojan incarnation for having taken his own life. Apparently the gates of Troy had been virtually impenetrable, and it was through the activities of an overly trusting soldier that the Trojan horse had been allowed into the city. That soldier had been Xenon, who lost face for his actions and committed suicide (294–183). Cayce's reading went on to suggest that this deed of "self-effacement" had to be met in the present, apparently through experiencing and then overcoming a series of failures in which Cayce himself had to find the faith and the motivation to continue on.

Out of the two thousand life readings that Cayce gave during his lifetime, some forty-five individuals were told that they had once lived during the period of the Trojan War. Although the vast majority were soldiers, wives, and guards whose names have not been remembered by history, in addition to Achilles two other personalities of note did make an appearance: the Trojan hero, Hector (5717-5); and Helen (136-1), the woman whose face would launch a thousand ships. In addition to an exploration of Troy, one of the interesting insights provided by the readings is how each of these individuals, including Cayce himself, had to contend with personal biases and inclinations from the past being played out in their experiences in the present.

Even though more than 3,000 years have passed since the events of the Trojan War took place, the story continues to inspire and fascinate much of humankind. The idea that some individuals may have had firsthand experiences during this period of human history is certainly intriguing, but the possibility that this tale encapsulates archetypal patterns of human behavior, hopes, and dreams that somehow provide meaning for countless individuals is perhaps even more significant. Truly, there is something about this story that captures the imagination.

This book has been compiled to explore the story of the Trojan War especially for those who might never themselves brave the epics of Homer and Virgil, the myths of ancient Greece, the investigations of Schliemann and other archaeologists, or even the life's work of Edgar

Cayce. In addition to providing individuals with an overview of the mythic tale and some of the archaeological research that followed, it will explore psychic information that has not previously been available to the general public. It will also examine some of the components of the story that may have been responsible for holding the interest of humanity for literally thousands of years.

Taken together, this is *Mythic Troy*, with insights from legend, history, and intuition.

# 1

# When There Were Gods

The religion of the Greeks was a mythology rich with legend, symbolism, and tales of heroism that attempted to explain everything about the human condition. Whether discussing the cycles of nature, the complexities of human emotion and passion, the apparent causes of tragedy or joy, or the seeming hand of fate and destiny, the Greeks assigned much significance to the activities of the gods and their ongoing involvement in complicating the affairs of humankind. The gods and goddesses of ancient Greece were very much a part of everyday life. In Greek philosophy, the varied kingdoms that made up the country of Greece were believed to be near the center of a world that was flat, and the very center of that world was Mount Olympus, the home of the gods.

1

The story of mythic Troy is inextricably woven with the Greeks' belief in these ancient deities. In fact, according to the tale, had it not been for the ongoing intervention and favoritism of the gods, the countries of Greece and Troy might never have gone to war. Or, at the very least, they might have eventually come to peaceful terms and enacted a lasting truce.

Rather than being all-powerful and benevolent, the gods of ancient times were believed to possess a special gift or focus in which they excelled; oftentimes, they were also fraught with their own desires, dreams, hopes, and fears. These gods were considered to be much like human beings—each with his or her strengths, weaknesses, and personality flaws. The Greeks believed that these gods and goddesses might or might not come to the aid of any mortal that beseeched them; actually, the fate of individuals often rested upon the whims of the immortals. Sometimes the characteristics of a particular god and his or her benevolence or mischievousness even depended upon the geographic region of the country. Deriving much of their philosophy from nature and its cycles, the Greeks believed in many gods and goddesses and attributed a variety of traits and mythic tales to them. Perhaps the greatest difference between these divine beings and human beings was simply that the gods were immortal.

In his book *The Origin of Consciousness in the Breakdown of the Bicameral Mind* (1976), Julian Jaynes presents the theory that the gods and goddesses of ancient times might have originated as an inner voice of consciousness that occurred during a stage in the evolutionary development of the human mind. Although his theory is somewhat controversial, Jaynes believes that this inner voice often occurred in the form of hallucinations that presented themselves when the right half of the brain sent auditory and visual information to the left half.

In looking back on this same period in history and describing the origins of the gods, the Edgar Cayce information states that these ancient deities were created as humankind attempted to understand the boundaries of nature. This understanding also extended to observing the natural forces that manifested themselves in the physical, the mental, and even the spiritual realms (900-17). The creation of a philosophy that attributed much to the gods and goddesses of the ancient world was essentially connected to humanity's desire to understand the universal laws at work in life. Ultimately, the forces that were assigned to these ancient deities could actually be attributed to aspects of the One God, the Creator of the universe. In the language of the Edgar Cayce readings:

> **All force has its incentive, the directing or creating of that force. That force to the human mind apparent, as different conditions, or relations, as referred to as the God, or the ruling force, of that individual force, as is giving the expression, and is referred to as the God, as of War, as of Peace, as of Water, as of the elements under the Sea. As of those above, as the God of High Heaven, the ruler over all, the one in all and the all in one.        3744-5**

According to Greek philosophy, in the beginning the universe was a "shapeless mass" devoid of light over which reigned a deity called Chaos and his wife Nyx (Guerber, pgs. 12–13). From this couple came Day (Hemera) and Light (Aether), who in turn gave birth to Eros (love), Gaea (the earth), and Pontus (the sea). In time, these early gods would give birth to twelve Titans—six divine men and six divine women. The youngest of the Titans was Cronus, who eventually conspired with Gaea to overthrow his own father and the rest of the early gods.

From Cronus and his sister-wife, Rhea, would come a number of gods, including Zeus, Poseidon, Hades, and Hera. Eventually, Zeus followed his parental example and overthrew his father to place himself in the position of supreme ruler. He then divided his power among his two brothers and married his sister. To Poseidon he gave the sea and all the waters of the earth; to Hades he gave the underworld. In spite of his marriage to Hera, Zeus was prone to frequent sexual alliances with all kinds of mortal and immortal women. As a result he had many children, some who became gods and goddesses themselves.

In Greek mythology the twelve chief gods were: Zeus (king of the gods), Hera (queen of the gods), Poseidon (god of the sea), Hades (god of the underworld), Aphrodite (goddess of love and beauty), Athena (goddess of wisdom), Apollo (god of prophecy), Hermes (messenger god), Artemis (goddess of hunting and chastity), Hestia (goddess of the hearth), Ares (the god of war), and Hephaestus (god of fire). These twelve individuals were related either as siblings or as parent–child, and they often vied for power and supremacy over each other. In time, Rome would adopt the individual characteristics of these same gods and goddesses, providing each with a Roman name, as follows:

| Greek Name | Roman Name |
|------------|------------|
| Zeus | Jupiter/Jove |
| Hera | Juno |
| Poseidon | Neptune |
| Hades | Pluto |
| Aphrodite | Venus |
| Athena | Minerva |
| Apollo | Apollo/Phoebus |
| Hermes | Mercury |
| Artemis | Diana |
| Hestia | Vesta |
| Ares | Mars |
| Hephaestus | Vulcan |

In addition to these major gods and goddesses was a host of minor deities, each with their own concerns and areas of activity, such as Cupid (Amor), the god of love; Demeter (Ceres), the goddess of agriculture; Dionysus (Bacchus), the god of wine; and many others. Beyond the gods and goddesses of the ancient world, lesser divine beings of Greek mythology included nine Muses, who presided over song, art, literature, and science; three Graces, responsible for social activities, such as banquet and dance; and the three sisters of Fate, who oversaw the course of human destiny (Bulfinch, pgs. 13–14). It is the Muses that the epic poet generally addresses at the beginning of a tale, thereby requesting their help and assistance in telling the story.

Greek mythology is important to the Trojan tale because, according to legend, some of the gods and goddesses were intricately involved in the Greek–Trojan conflict. In addition to helping instigate the war, once conflict was underway some of these ancient deities apparently chose sides, lending their support, influence, and power to one country or another.

The degree of the gods' involvement in the Trojan War depends upon the manner in which the legend is told. Accordingly, the ultimate blame for the conflict also varies and can be arguably traced to Eris, a lesser goddess of discord, to Zeus, to Poseidon, to Aphrodite, or perhaps even to Hera. Conversely, the mortal blame might be placed upon individuals such as Paris, prince of Troy; Helen, an illegitimate daughter of Zeus from his alliance with Leda; or even Odysseus. Ultimately, however, an entire chain of events may have been responsible for the warfare between Greece and Troy.

As background information, Greek mythology states that Ilus, who was the son of Tros, founded Troy. Ilus named the city of Troy after his father and hired the help of Apollo and Poseidon to build the city's great walls. Because Ilus founded the city, on some occasions Troy is also referred to as Ilium. Unfortunately, after the city was complete, Ilus cheated the gods out of their rightful payment, which led to the city being without divine protection and ultimately to its first attack during the reign of Ilus' son, Laomedon. Because he had been cheated, the god Poseidon became a sworn enemy of Troy, and the city and its people became vulnerable to attack from any mortal enemy.

Because of Poseidon's wrath, each year the god sent a sea monster to wreak havoc upon the city. On each occasion the sea monster was only appeased when the city presented a virgin that could be devoured. The sacrifice was made annually until the time came that the lot fell to King Laomedon's daughter. Rather than giving up his daughter, Laomedon sought help from Hercules and offered this legendary hero the city's immortal, snow white horses in exchange for the death of the monster. The Trojans were known for their horses, which were considered among the country's prized possessions. Although Hercules killed the monster with his mighty bow and arrow, Laomedon reneged on his promise. As a result, Hercules attacked the city, killing Laomedon in the process. Laomedon's son, Priam, was put in charge because he made good on his father's debt and paid Hercules the horses that had been demanded. Hercules also took Priam's sister, Hesione, as part of his payment.

Years passed and King Priam and his wife, Hecuba, successfully ruled the Trojan throne. The day came when Hecuba was about to have another child. In all, the couple would have a total of at least forty-nine children, including Hector (their eldest son, according to some accounts), heir to the kingdom, and Cassandra, a woman who was wooed by Apollo and to whom the god had given the gift of prophecy. Some accounts suggest that the prolific couple actually had sixty-two children: fifty sons and twelve daughters. During this particular pregnancy, however, Hecuba had a dream that indicated her child would be a son who would eventually cause the death of his father and the destruction of the entire Trojan city. Seeking corroboration of the dream, Hecuba went to an oracle who also confirmed the prophecy. Consequently, when the child was born, he was abandoned on a mountainside to perish in order to avert the prediction. Rather than dying, however, the child was found by a sheepherder, who adopted the child as his own, named him Paris, and raised the boy to become a shepherd. By all accounts, Paris would grow to be an extremely handsome lad. He remained ignorant of his royal birth for many years. In fact, his life as a shepherd was seemingly blissful, and he was loved by and married to the nymph Œnone, whom he would later abandon in his search for Helen.

While this chain of events was transpiring in Troy, Zeus began courting a woman named Leda, who was already married to King Tyndareus of Sparta. In order to win her charms, Zeus disguised himself in the form of a beautiful swan. The sexual union between these two resulted in the birth of Helen. As Helen grew to adulthood, she became one of the most beautiful women in the world. She was so desirable that men from all over Greece sought her favors and asked for her hand in marriage, although Helen turned them all down. Because of the vast number of suitors, it was feared that the day might come when one of those who had been rejected would return to kidnap her. For that reason, according to some versions of the tale, Odysseus, who was leader of the Greek kingdom of Ithaca, came up with a proposal.

Odysseus himself had once courted and been rejected by Helen. Afterwards, he had married her cousin, Penelope. Nonetheless, he believed that Helen's desirability would lead to trouble unless steps were taken to avert the problem. He proposed an alliance that became known as the Oath of Tyndareus. (In some versions, it was Tyndareus who actually made the proposal.) Unfortunately, the alliance was one of the events that eventually unified all of the smaller kingdoms of Greece against the people of Troy. According to Greek mythology, the idea of the oath occurred as follows:

> **Helen had many suitors who ardently strove to win her favor. The noblest, bravest, and best came to woo and hoped to win; but all were left in suspense, as the maiden did not show any preference, and refused to make known her choice.**
>
> **Tyndareus, Helen's stepfather, thinking the rejected suitors might attempt to steal her away from any husband she selected, proposed that all the candidates for her hand should take a solemn oath, binding themselves to respect the marital rights of the favored suitor, and help him regain possession of his wife should any one venture to kidnap her. (Guerber, pg. 311)**

Eventually, all of Helen's previous suitors took the oath, and Helen finally turned her favors to an individual named Menelaus. The two married and, in time, Menelaus would inherit the kingdom of Sparta from his father-in-law.

The next event that would eventually seal Troy's fate occurred when Zeus became enamored with Thetis, a beautiful sea nymph. The god was so taken by her beauty that he planned to marry her. However, prior to their marriage, Zeus sought the advice of the sisters of Fate. The three predicted that Thetis would give birth to a son whose destiny was to become more powerful than his father. Not wanting to be usurped by his own child, Zeus decided to give the hand of Thetis in marriage to a mortal; he chose Peleus, the king of Athens.

Although Thetis was somewhat disheartened by the fact that she was to be married to a mere mortal, Zeus promised the wedding would be such cause for celebration that even the gods themselves would be in attendance. Finally, Thetis agreed to the match. True to his word, Zeus arrived with all the gods except for one. According to the tale, Eris, the goddess of discord, was not invited because of her foul mood and her unpleasant temperament. In addition to the gods and goddesses, all of Athens arrived for the ceremony.

Just when the wedding was about to begin and all the guests had taken their seats, Eris surprised everyone by entering the banquet hall uninvited. Many feared that she had come to seek revenge for being omitted from the party. Without speaking a word, however, she walked over to the banquet table and threw down a solid gold apple inscribed with three simple words: "To the Fairest." With that, she departed.

At first, quite a few of the women attending the wedding appeared anxious to claim the prize as their own—human and immortal alike. However, those most persistent at arguing their respective claims as "the fairest" were Hera, Aphrodite, and Athena. These three continually argued amongst themselves for the prize. Their arguments persisted for so long that eventually all other claimants had given up. But these three persisted—none being willing to surrender the apple to the other two. Hera believed that she alone, as queen of the gods, rightly deserved the prize. Aphrodite was confident that she, as goddess of beauty, deserved the honor. Athena, as goddess of wisdom, was certain that wisdom and intellect made her the fairest of them all.

The argument among them heightened to such an extent that the wedding was interrupted. Eventually, the three goddesses called upon the wedding guests to solve the dispute, but no one wanted to make the decision, fearing that the two who failed to receive the prize would seek retribution against the one who made the choice. Finally, the three goddesses became desperate to find someone to make the decision, so they turned to Zeus. Zeus himself refused to decide the contest and instead sent them to the nearby mountaintop of Mount Ida (with the apple) to resolve the dispute. As fate would have it, Paris was tending his flocks upon the same mountain when the goddesses arrived. The three came to the handsome, young shepherd and appointed him to choose the fairest.

To influence his choice, each of the three promised to give Paris every manner of reward and favor. Hera promised to bestow him with wealth and unlimited power. Athena swore she would provide him with the gift of untold wisdom. Finally, Aphrodite pledged that she would give the young man a wife as beautiful as herself in exchange for the coveted prize. Being greatly affected by Aphrodite's beauty, Paris gave the golden apple to her without hesitation. Aphrodite was delighted. Unfortunately, both Hera and Athena became his sworn enemies. The two goddesses vowed to wait until the time was right to seek their revenge.

In payment of her promise, Aphrodite told Paris of his royal birthright and instructed him to return to Troy in order to obtain a fleet of ships from his parents, the king and queen. Afterwards he was to sail to Greece where he would find Helen, his promised bride, who was the wife of King Menelaus of Sparta. Following Aphrodite's instructions, Paris eventually returned to Troy during a festival that involved the entire kingdom. Rather than exposing his identity, Paris took part in the athletic games during the festivities and made a name for himself as a man of skill and bravery.

As fate would have it, during the games Paris was spotted by his sister, Cassandra. She told her parents that the young man's appearance was identical to that of her brothers, making her certain that he was the royal couple's long-lost son. She also foretold that this young man was destined to bring destruction upon the entire city. Unfortunately, although Cassandra possessed the gift of prophecy, her predictions were constantly ignored. Apollo had bestowed this gift upon her as a means of winning her favor, and the gods could not take back a power once it had been given. Because her relationship with Apollo had not worked out, he willed that those who heard her prophecies would simply ignore them. For this reason, the king and queen chastised their daughter for her prediction. Instead, delighted at seeing their son Paris, they restored him to his proper place in the palace and promised to grant him every wish to atone for their long neglect. Together, they vowed to make amends for abandoning him as a babe.

When the time was right, Paris told King Priam that he wanted to sail to Greece to recover his father's sister, Hesione, who had been taken by Hercules. In truth, however, Paris simply used the plan that Aphrodite had suggested. Nonetheless, the falsehood worked, and Priam provided Paris with several ships, which he directed to Menelaus' kingdom in Greece.

Upon his arrival at the home of Menelaus and Helen in Sparta, Paris was greeted as a royal guest and treated as a visiting dignitary. For ten days he received his host's splendid hospitality until, at last, Menelaus was called away on business to Crete. King Menelaus asked his wife to continue to care for their guest during his absence. Once Paris was left alone with Helen, the prince of Troy began to court her.

To be sure, Helen's participation in the seduction has long been cause for much speculation. According to some, Paris abducted her along with much of Menelaus' treasure and returned to Troy, keeping her as a virtual prisoner. Others suggest that Helen was all too willing to become the captive and concubine of this handsome Trojan prince. Some contend that her willingness was only due to the fact that she had been brainwashed and influenced by Aphrodite as a means of fulfilling the goddess's oath to Paris. In any event, when Menelaus returned and discovered his wife's absence, he became convinced that she had been kidnapped against her will. Immediately, he went to his brother Agamemnon for help. At first the two tried diplomacy with Troy, requesting Helen's swift return. Only when their calls went unanswered did Menelaus enlist the aid of the other Greek kings and warriors by invoking the Oath of Tyndareus. As all of Helen's former suitors were called into battle to retrieve her, the stage became set for a war between the kingdom of Troy and the various city-state kingdoms of Greece. However, it would be ten years before any fighting between Greece and Troy actually occurred.

Legend suggests that two years after the abduction of Helen, the Greek forces originally landed at a place called Mysia, which they had mistaken for Troy. There the Greeks were beaten by King Telephus and forced to return to their homeland. It would be another eight years before the Greek forces would gather again and prepare to attack the Trojans. Thus, Helen would have been in captivity as the wife of Paris for ten years before the Trojan War had even started.

# 2

# LET THERE BE WAR

From the very beginning, Achilles and Odysseus, two of Greek's most prominent warrior–leaders, refused to heed the call to arms because of prophecies that had warned each not to participate in the Trojan conflict. According to legend, Achilles had long known that his participation would mean death, not glory. Odysseus had been warned that if he took part in the war it would be twenty years before he saw his home again.

In the case of Achilles, although his mother, the sea nymph Thetis, was an immortal, he was not. Knowing that the boy was destined to become a great warrior, she took him as a baby to the river Styx where she held him by the heel and dipped him in the magical waters to give him some manner of protection. In Greek mythology, the river Styx was in Hades and served as a place where the gods swore their most solemn oaths. Her deed made Achilles invulnerable, except in the heel by which she had held him.

Later, an oracle predicted that Achilles would in fact die from a wound in his heel within the shadow of the walls of Troy. Thetis vowed that her son would never experience such a fate and had him trained by the centaur (half man and half horse) Chiron to become the greatest warrior and hero of all time. Shortly after the training, there were rumors of war between Greece and Troy. To prevent Achilles from going to battle and meeting the fate that had been prophesied, Thetis had her son sent to the court of King Lycomedes disguised as a woman, so he could avoid the call to arms.

To possibly gain insights into the historical character of Achilles' mother, we'll turn to the Cayce psychic readings. In September 1927, a thirty-six-year-old saleswoman in a stock brokerage office was told in a reading from Edgar Cayce that in a previous incarnation she had been the mother of Achilles. Several interesting facts are suggested by the Cayce information in this regard. In the first place, rather than implying that Achilles' mother had been a legendary immortal, the reading states that his mother had been a flesh-and-blood individual. In that lifetime she became known for her independence, her innate capacity to achieve whatever goal she had in mind, and her ability to rule and guide men as individuals, as well as women in groups. Oftentimes, Edgar Cayce would tell people who obtained past-life readings both what they had gained and had lost in terms of soul development during their previous incarnations, and the mother of Achilles was no exception. In the language of the Cayce information, the present-day saleswoman learned the following:

> **In the one before this we find in that period when there were the wars in that time when Achilles ruled in that land. The entity then one who gave much to the strength and power to the entity, being then in the flesh the mother of Achilles [now Mr. (900)], and ruling in power through the tenets given to the entity in that period— and losing in self through the aggrandizement of power, position, and the tenets of earth's surroundings. In the urge is seen that of**

the ability to guide or rule men, and the same in the ability to guide or rule women, yet *one* in the individual, the other rather in groups.                                                                302-1

Interestingly enough, the reading confirms the fact that Achilles' mother was instrumental in helping the warrior develop his "strength and power," as suggested by legend. In addition, the brokerage company in which Miss [302] worked in this lifetime was owned by Mr. [900], whom the readings identified as the reincarnation of Achilles.

In a follow-up reading given to the twenty-nine-year-old man that Cayce identified as Achilles, the information confirms how Achilles' mother raised him to become an outstanding warrior, as well as making certain that he was well connected both politically and socially. It also substantiates the legendary account that this celebrated warrior had received his armor from his mother:

The entity [Achilles] then as the male offspring and entered in with the beauties of the rustic nature of the time and place, near Athenia or Athens, and raised to manhood, or young manhood, in and about the Mount, and given all advantages in the exercises and games and learning of the day, with the beauties of that in that day as could be obtained by one that was raised for the special purpose of entering into the political, social and other conditions of day and age. Soon learned that of the soldier with the spear, bow and axe, with an armor as prepared by the mother of the body, and given all the benefits of the aristocrats of the age, given exceptional abilities and applied same in the moral, physical, development of the body. One, then, beautiful of stature, physical, mind and of the expressing of same. Soon drawn in early manhood into the political situations surrounding the conditions of the country, coming then as a companion to many of the leaders in that day when there were personal combats in every phase of the physical prowess of the body. The entity showing the exceptional abilities of the environments under which the body had been developed in the day when this, the development of physical prowess, was studied and given the greater extent of attention. In personal combats often the body [was] successful and called the leader of the army and group, or the personal representative of the armies of the entity in the reign of those in charge of same at time.                                                                    900-63

In the present, Mr. [900] found himself deeply attracted to the woman that had once been his mother. At the same time, a number of individuals had warned him to handle her "with kid gloves," since she seemed intent on getting ahead in business using whatever means she could. In writing Mr. Cayce about his relationship with this young woman, Mr. [900] confessed his feelings as follows:

Now regarding [Miss 302]. You and Mrs. Cayce may feel somehow that you would rather steer shy. For a while I felt that way and she sort of backed me to the wall . . . [However] I know that if she will seek to apply her power for good, as well as monetary gain, she will do for our institute work what she has done for our business—i.e., simply build it up right. She has a personality that rules—is as a mighty queen of old, and men and women all seek her favor . . . she uses sex appeal only to trap men, then making them feel ashamed of themselves, and feel that she is placing on them the responsibility not only of redeeming themselves, but of honoring themselves in her sight by bringing her needed aid financially . . .

Why then do I defend her cause, or care more than for the business end? My desire to carry out my ideal of helping each one help himself for the benefit of a higher civilization? Yes, I inherit from a past incarnation the desire to help others, particularly the lowly, but even aside from that—is there something intuitive of the mother she once was to me that I am defending? Probably I'll get more of this later. On her part sometimes I think she'd like to treat me like a child, or son, yet other times the purely physical takes possession and then she'd like to see me get in line with the others. She oscillates back and forth even as she does with her power, seeing no other way of using it than to make people bring her ma-

**terial success. If she could only see the further greater use of it—
how wonderful to lift people up who are bowed down with grief,
sickness, misfortune and cares and inspire them to fight their way
to better conditions—how wonderful to create in men the influence to do good, kindly, noble and gentle deeds that will bring
happiness into the heart and mind of humanity.**

**302-3 Background Report**

According to reports on file with the Cayce archives, within a couple
of years Miss [302] left her employment at the brokerage firm and began
working for a manufacturing company. A routine mailing from Cayce's
secretary to her in 1938 was returned "address unknown."

Greek legend continues with the tale of Odysseus, describing how
the warrior at first avoided the call to war. Apparently, Odysseus had no
desire to go into combat and risk not being able to return for two decades. Instead, he decided to remain at home in Ithaca, admiring his
wife, Penelope (who was Helen's cousin), and spending time with his
young son, Telemachus. When the king's messenger, Palamedes, arrived
in Ithaca to invoke the Oath of Tyndareus, Odysseus pretended to be
insane as a guise for avoiding the battle.

Some accounts contend that Odysseus pretended to be mad by sow-
ing salt into his own fields. Others suggest that he yoked an ox to a
plow and began plowing the sands of the seashore. In either event, the
king's messenger believed that Odysseus was trying to outsmart him.
For that reason, Palamedes took Odysseus' infant, Telemachus, and
threw him in front of the blades of the plow. Odysseus turned the ox
and plow aside very quickly and skillfully and avoided harming his
son. For that reason, Palamedes knew that Odysseus had complete control of his senses. Since the warrior was not insane, he was forced to
obey the call to arms.

Odysseus arrived as the army gathered under King Agamemnon—
brother to King Menelaus. The troops included some of the most outstanding Greek warriors of the day. In addition to Odysseus, there was
the elderly warrior Nestor, known for his wise counsel, and two of
Greece's greatest warriors and heroes (besides Achilles and Odysseus),

Ajax and Diomedes. Legend suggests that it took years for all of the Greek forces to gather from the various city–states in the port of Aulis, and then to regroup after their erroneous assault on Mysia.

In 1930, Edgar Cayce told a forty–one–year–old music teacher that she had been among those individuals who served as rulers over the independent Greek city–states. Although the reading does not clearly indicate whether she or her people took part in the conflict, it does place her tenure as leader at the period of the early build–up to war. It also suggests that her personal interests at the time took precedence over anything else that might have demanded her time and resources:

> **In the one before this we find in that period known as the Trojan War, in the extreme beginning of same, when there was the changing of the peoples from the isle to the mainlands and the building up of those in that portion known as the lower portion of Grecian country at present. Then did the entity *rule*, as it were, with an indomitable and impregnable will, and many were they that found the displeasure of the entity to their own undoing. In the name Helois. In this experience the entity gained and lost; gained in the abilities to have the opportunity to have been of aid; lost in the aggrandizing of selfish interests as brought to the beautiful body, to the wonderful mind, those who sought for favor and were granted not.                                                    1918-1**

Some accounts suggest that the Greek troops that assembled numbered many tens of thousands, perhaps even fifty thousand or more! Hundreds of years later the magnitude of the Greek force would be immortalized in a line from Christopher Marlowe's *Doctor Faustus* (ca. 1589) where referring to Helen of Troy the question was posed: "Was this the face that launch'd a thousand ships and burnt the topless towers of Ilium [Troy]?"

Before the combined forces of the Greek armies departed for Troy, however, Kalchas, the Greek soothsayer and oracle, was consulted to prophesy the outcome of the war. Kalchas predicted that it would take ten years of conflict before the walls of Troy fell. The soothsayer also informed Menelaus, Agamemnon, and the others that Troy could never be defeated without the aid of Achilles, who remained in hiding. For that reason, one messenger after another was sent to find Achilles, and all returned without success. Finally, it was left to the wise and shrewd Odysseus to discover Achilles' whereabouts.

Odysseus sensed that Achilles was somehow hiding in the court of King Lycomedes. To outsmart Achilles, Odysseus dressed himself in the garb of a traveling peddler and journeyed to the home of Lycomedes with a sack of wares in tow. The sack contained many trinkets and ornaments, but several pieces of weaponry had been hidden within the bottom of the sack as well. As the disguised Odysseus emptied his sack and displayed his wares to the women of the court, he watched each of them closely. One after another, the women fondled and admired the trinkets that had been put out for them to see. However, one of the women chose instead to handle the weapons that the others had totally disregarded. In fact, the woman brandished the weaponry with such skill and bravery that it became clear to Odysseus that he had found Achilles. Once the disguise was uncovered, Odysseus eloquently persuaded his countryman to join the others in war. Unfortunately, once Achilles and Odysseus journeyed to rejoin the others, they discovered that the Greek army had suddenly been visited with two enormous problems. The first was an inexplicable plague that had killed a number of the Greek forces; and the second was that no winds were blowing in port, completely crippling the Greek ships where they lay docked.

Once again the oracle Kalchas was summoned to explain the turn of events. According to the soothsayer, it was the goddess Artemis (Diana) who was angry with Agamemnon and had visited both the pestilence and the lack of wind upon the army. Apparently, during the time that the troops had been gathering, the Greek king had gone hunting and inadvertently killed a deer that was sacred to the goddess. Kalchas suggested that there could be but one remedy to appease the goddess's wrath: a virgin had to be sacrificed upon her altar. The oracle then stated that the virgin the goddess preferred was Iphigenia, King Agamemnon's own daughter.

Although he was reluctant, King Agamemnon was eventually per-

suaded that he had no other choice. With the passage of time the pestilence had not abated nor had the winds returned. With that in mind,
Agamemnon sent word to his daughter that before his departure he
wanted to attend her wedding ceremony. In order to bring her to the
place of sacrifice, the king lied that Achilles had been chosen to be her
husband and her presence at the port of Aulis was requested immediately. When word reached Iphigenia, she was ecstatic and came as
quickly as possible:

> **Iphigenia came to her father secretly delighted at being the cho-
> sen bride of such a hero; but, instead of being led to the hymeneal
> altar, she was dragged to the place of sacrifice, where the priest,
> with uplifted knife, was about to end her sufferings, when Diana
> [Artemis] suddenly appeared, snatched her up in a cloud, and left
> in her stead a deer, which was duly sacrificed, while Iphigenia was
> borne in safety to Tauris, where she became a priestess in one of
> the goddess's temples. (Guerber, pg. 316)**

While some legends confirm that Artemis came and rescued
Iphigenia to become a priestess in one of her temples, others state that
the young woman was actually put to death. In any event, immediately
thereafter the winds returned and the Greek fleet sailed in the direction
of Troy.

According to the Trojan Myth, the first Greek to step foot on the
shoreline was Protesilaus, who was killed the instant his foot touched
the soil. (Some accounts state that it was Hector who killed him.) Almost
immediately news of his death reached back home to the ears of his
wife, Laodamia. She was so depressed that she begged the gods to let
her have just one further conversation with him. So moved were the
gods by her touching request that they instructed Hermes (Mercury),
the messenger god, to take Protesilaus back to earth for three hours so
that he and his wife could converse.

Laodamia was overjoyed to see him. For three hours the two of them
were able to speak with one another. During that time Protesilaus described the details of his death, and the couple discussed their love for

one another. Finally, when the three hours were up, Hermes returned to conduct Protesilaus back to Hades. Immediately after his departure, Laodamia herself died of grief in order to remain with her husband.

Relative to the start of the war, Edgar Cayce told an individual in 1927 that in a previous lifetime during the onset of the Trojan War he had guided the boat that carried Achilles to the shoreline. For his support of Achilles he later gained power and favor but misused that power to the apparent detriment of his own soul development. The reading suggests that the Greeks had taken control of the Trojan port before moving on to take the city itself:

> **In the one before this we find in that land when Achilles ruled in the port, and the entity then guided the barque that brought Achilles to the shores of the besieged city, and the entity gained favor, and lost through the misapplication of power given by that ruler. Then in the name of Sansan, and the entity brought good and bad to self and others through the misapplication of power and position, and in the urge as is seen, the fear that those in power will not acknowledge the efforts of the entity. Rid self of such, for in power there is the application of strength. Strength and power are *not* the same. In the application there may power and strength attained from either.                                                                        2694-1**

Legend states that the Trojan War officially began with the death of Protesilaus and would continue for many years to come. During that time, countless casualties were suffered on both sides; however, neither side proved victorious over the other. For nine long years, every attempt by the Greeks to enter the walled city of Troy was averted. During that same period, however, the Trojans were unable to drive the Greeks from their shoreline. As time passed and the war entered its tenth year, the battle appeared to be in a standoff.

It is at this point in the Trojan Myth that the story of Homer's *Iliad* actually begins.

# 3

# THE TROJAN MYTH AND THE *ILIAD*

**A**ccording to the *Iliad*, for nine long years the battle between the Greeks and the Trojans raged on with neither side becoming the decisive victor. Although the Greek armies under the direction of King Agamemnon and the lead warrior Achilles had overtaken neighboring cities and various allies of the Trojan people, because of the strength of the Trojan army as well as the city's stone walls, the city itself had remained un–harmed.

Legend suggests that part of the reason the city remained un–harmed was due to its outer walls and perhaps even a system of inner walls that surrounded the entire city of Troy and protected all the inhabitants from attack. Beginning with the excavations of Heinrich Schliemann in the late nineteenth century[5], it became apparent that at various periods in history walls did encircle the city. As early as 1881, Schliemann wrote about his excavation of the city wall by stating:

> **I further excavated to the east and southeast of the "Great Tower" . . . in order to unearth the city wall and its connection with the two gigantic stone walls called by me "the Great Tower." All of this has been accomplished. My excavations to the south, southwest, west, northwest, and north of the gates, have also enabled me to uncover the city wall in these directions; so that it is now disclosed in its entire circuit, except where is has been cut through by my great trench. (Schliemann, pg. 54)**

The existence of such a complex of walls suggests that sufficient warriors and guards would need to be in place simply to maintain the city's security. With this in mind, it is interesting that the Cayce information told a number of individuals that during a previous incarnation at the time of the Trojan War they had been guards or attendants to guards who had been stationed to protect the city gates and walls. For example, in 1930, a forty-two-year-old salesman was told that twice during former lifetimes he had served in the capacity of a soldier. In addition to being involved with the French Revolution, during the Trojan period he had been one of those responsible for the gates on the eastern wall of the city. Apparently, his adverse experience at the time had remained with him at a soul level, causing a present-day tendency to be critical of authority figures:

> **In the one before this in that period known as the Trojan period, the entity again the soldier—and among those who builded in the gates in the eastern side, and standing with those that defied the armies from without; gaining and losing through this experience. In the name Saladbid. In the application of the experience in the**

---

[5]See also chapter on Heinrich Schliemann and Archaeological Research at Troy.

present, is the many changes in ideas and ideals, and those who
would be in power are as persecutors to those not so favored in
the world's goods, or in positions, and the entity then becomes of
that nature or tendency where it *decries* those that are in political
power, or in power as rulers, judges, justices, and such.    1728-2

During the same year, parents of an eight-year-old mentally handi-
capped boy were told that their son had once been one of the guards
who controlled the gates. In that capacity, the youth had been one of
those ultimately responsible for deciding who would be let in and out
of Troy. Edgar Cayce suggested that one of the strengths the boy had
acquired during that period was maintaining an openness and an understanding of the various non-Trojan people, groups, and cultures that
visited the walled city:

> ... when in that period known as the Trojan the entity was among
> the sources of the communicative forces with those as controlled
> the egress, and the going in and coming out of the peoples; being,
> then, among those in the guard in same, and a figure to be reck-
> oned with in physical prowess, in mental speculation . . . in the
> service of those less fortunate, or even upon the same plane of
> experience; for the entity gained in that, without thought of self,
> without thought of other than attempting to give an understand-
> ing of many in varied groups, the entity aided much.       758-23

A thirty-eight-year-old merchant learned that his present-day tendency of being committed to a purpose had its foundations during his
experience as a dedicated Trojan guard and defender of the gate:

> In the one before this we find in that period known as the Trojan
> period. The entity then among those of the defenders at the gate,
> and in that experience the entity the first and second guard at the
> gate, known in the name as Hault. The entity gained through this
> experience, for the entity gave not only self but the *mind* of self to
> a purpose, a cause, held as uppermost in the mind and the experi-

ence of the entity. In the present, the defense of that held as truth,
as purposeful, will the entity defend to the last; whether with body,
with physical, or with *material* gain.                              99-6

Suggesting that the guards were seldom able to leave their posts, a
twenty-two-year-old woman was told in 1927 that she had been one of
those who "ministered" to the various city gatekeepers:

> In the one before this we find in that Trojan period when there was
> war made in the land and the city was besieged. The entity then
> among those who ministered especially to the keepers at the gates.
> Then in the name Pamn, and the entity gained through this experi-
> ence, finding much in peoples, positions, conditions, to study and
> wonder about; yet keeping true to that desire set in self—to re-
> main unspotted from the world though beset on every hand, yet
> remaining true in every sense to self and to others. Gaining, then,
> through this experience.                                          369-3

Edgar Cayce also told a twenty-five-year-old dietician that she had
been one of those who had brought food to the gatekeepers. During
that lifetime, she was apparently captured by the attacking forces after
the death of her husband and taken as a concubine—an experience
that, understandably, had caused her to become angry and resentful:

> In the one before this we find in that land known as the Trojan
> land, and during those periods when there was the guarding of the
> gates. The entity showed forth most of that that had to do with the
> development of, or retarding of, the experience—in the name
> Elois. The entity among those who furnished foods for the keepers
> of the gates, and the companion—or the wife, then—of one of the
> keepers, and in the experience the entity gained. Losing only in
> the grudge held when the companion losing life in the defense of
> the city, when changed to that of the companion of those who car-
> ried the entity away, the entity fought, grudged, and lost in the
> conditions builded in that of fear, temper, and the exaltation of

> same. In the present we find those conditions in the entity of fear
> as to outcomes, rather of divisions of peoples and of peoples' rela-
> tionships; yet in that of the building of the grudges, this the entity
> keeps apart. 1730-1

A thirty–nine–year–old woman was told that she had also "lost" in her Trojan experience. Although she had also gained at a soul level during the experience, she had lost because of "grudges held" against her attackers:

> In the one before this we find in that period when there were dis-
> cernments between the peoples of the island and those of the main-
> land, during that known as the Trojan period. The entity then
> among those that assisted those in the defense of the gate through
> which those armies overran the city. The entity gained and lost
> and gained through this sojourn. Then in the name Ialea. The en-
> tity through this experience, as felt in the present, the fear—and
> the war has often made changes, as it did here, close to, and an
> attendant of, and the companion of, the defender at the left gate.
> The entity lost through grudges held. This far from that felt in the
> present experience. 993-1

In Homer's account of the story, it was during the tenth year of the war that an argument between Agamemnon and Achilles threatened to undermine the entire Greek army. The argument was due to the capture of two beautiful young female captives who had been taken prisoner by the Greek forces while raiding one of the neighboring towns. The girls were named Chryseis and Briseis. Because he was chief king, Agamemnon was awarded Chryseis, and Achilles, as the greatest war-rior, received Briseis. As the legend goes, Chryseis' father was one of the chief priests of the god Apollo and was deeply upset by his daughter's imprisonment. Although the priest begged for his daughter's return and offered a handsome reward in exchange for the girl, Agamemnon re-fused. Therefore the priest prayed to Apollo that the god would make the Greeks relent to his request and Apollo answered by sending a pestilence to the Greek camp. For ten days a plague inflicted the troops, resulting in the death of many warriors and the disillusionment of the entire army.

After ten days, Achilles became desperate because Agamemnon had done nothing to counteract the plague. Essentially usurping the chief king's authority, Achilles called an assembly of the warriors himself. He also called the Greek soothsayer Kalchas to be in attendance. In front of the assembly Achilles asked Kalchas to describe why the army had been inflicted with the plague. The oracle responded that it was punishment from Apollo for Agamemnon's refusal to return the maiden Chryseis to her father.

After the announcement, Agamemnon became enraged at having been publicly named for being responsible for the pestilence. He agreed to return the priest's daughter but only on the condition that she would be replaced with Briseis, the maiden originally awarded to Achilles. Because of the chief king's demand, Achilles felt disrespected and humiliated, as he believed Briseis was actually his. In response to the king, Achilles threatened to withdraw himself and his forces from all further combat.

Nonetheless, Agamemnon completely ignored the threat. The king returned Chryseis to her father and sent for Briseis as a means of demonstrating that he was still the commander-in-chief, even over Achilles.

Achilles became outraged at how he had been treated. Feeling humiliated, the warrior prayed to his mother Thetis that she might intervene with the gods and somehow convince Zeus to allow the Trojans to defeat the Greeks. Thetis followed her son's request and visited Zeus, who, in turn, promised to help the Trojans even though his own wife Hera remained their bitter enemy.

Fulfilling his promise, Zeus assisted the Trojans by sending a false dream to King Agamemnon. The dream was untrue, from a messenger who claimed to represent Zeus and who also suggested a Greek victory was at hand:

> **You should not sleep all night, not as a captain responsible for his men, with many duties, a great voice in the conferences of war.**

> Follow me closely: I am a messenger from Zeus, who is far away but holds you dear. "Prepare the troops," he said, "to take the field without delay: now may you take by storm the spacious town of Troy. The Olympian gods are of two minds no longer: Hera's pleading swayed them all, and bitter days from Zeus await the Trojans." Hold on to this message against forgetfulness in tides of day when blissful sleep is gone. (Fitzgerald, *Iliad*, Book Two, lines 28-40)

So inspired was Agamemnon by the dream that he decided to lead a mass assault on Troy. However, in order to test the commitment of his troops before ordering the assault, Agamemnon falsely announced that he believed his men had been fighting long enough and that they should all give up and go home. To his horror and surprise, the troops immediately broke rank and prepared their ships for the journey back to Greece. The warriors were tired of fighting. Only the intervention of the goddess Athena convinced the Greeks to stay.

As Agamemnon's troops began to scatter, Athena went to Odysseus and convinced him that it was right to fight the Trojans rather than leaving Helen behind. Because of her intervention, Odysseus announced to the Greek forces that the only honorable thing would be to remain and fight. Nestor, the wisest and oldest of all the Greek warriors, agreed with Odysseus and as a result of the stance and the intercession of the two men, the Greek army remained and prepared for attack.

As preparations began, Agamemnon recounted in extensive detail the lineage of the numerous forces that made up the Greek army, as well as the number of ships under their various commands. All told, legend has it that a thousands ships were under Greek command and included 50,000 men or more.

Meanwhile, the goddess Iris (messenger goddess in the *Iliad*) went to Hector to warn him that the Greeks were assembling for battle. Immediately after receiving the message, Hector ordered his own troops to meet the Greeks on the Trojan plains in front of the walled city. As the two armies advanced toward one another, Paris finally stepped forward and challenged any Greek who would fight him to a duel as a means of settling the war. As it turned out, Menelaus himself accepted the challenge and stepped forward, hoping to personally avenge his wife's abduction. Immediately, however, Paris became afraid and withdrew from the challenge.

Hector became upset and disgraced by his brother's behavior and called him a coward. After all, Paris had refused to fight the man that he himself had wronged. Because of the criticism, Paris believed that he had no choice but to follow through on his challenge. As a result, Agamemnon and Hector agreed that whoever won the battle between Menelaus and Paris would automatically win the war. It was decided that the victor would receive Helen as a prize and peace between the two countries could finally be declared.

The two warriors came together in hand–to–hand combat and in the process Menelaus proved victorious. Paris was wounded. However, before the Trojan prince could be killed, Aphrodite miraculously intervened. She magically carried Paris back to Troy in a mist and placed him safely in his bedroom with Helen.

Although Helen had been influenced by Aphrodite's power, Paris may not have been holding her entirely against her will. According to the story, sometimes the two acted more as sparring lovers rather than as captor and slave—in fact, the two would be together as husband and wife for twenty years. After Paris was miraculously transported from the battlefield back to his bedroom, Helen seemed irritated to see him:

> "Home from war? You should have perished there, brought down by that strong soldier, once my husband. You used to say you were the better man, more skillful with your hands, your spear. So why not challenge him to fight again?
>
> "I wouldn't if I were you. No, don't go back to war against the tawny-headed man of war like a rash fool. You'd crumple under his lance."
>
> Paris replied: "Love, don't be bitter with me. These are unkind reflections. It is true, on this occasion he—and Athena—won. Next time, I may. We, too, have gods with us. Let us drop war now, you and I, and give ourselves to pleasure in our bed. My soul was

never so possessed by longing . . . desire now lifts me like a tide."

He went to bed, and she went with him, and in the inlaid ivory
bed these two made love, while Menelaus roamed the ranks like a
wild beast, hunting the godlike man [Paris, who had disappeared
in the mist] . . . (Fitzgerald, *Iliad*, Book Three, lines 518-532,
537-541)

After Paris disappeared from the battlefield, Agamemnon declared
Menelaus the victor and claimed that Helen was rightfully theirs; however, the Trojans made no move to surrender their captive.

Tired of conflict, Zeus proposed that the nine-year war be brought to
a close. Unfortunately, both Hera and Athena disliked the idea and
would settle for nothing less than the complete and total annihilation
of Troy. For that reason, Hera begged Zeus to allow Athena to visit the
warfront and arranged for the Trojans to break the truce. According to
Homer, this was just one of many truces that had been proposed between the two rivals.

Interestingly enough, famed psychic Edgar Cayce told several individuals that they had literally been among those individuals who had
tried to mediate the dispute between Greece and Troy. In one instance,
a thirty-six-year-old attorney was told that his present day abilities to
mediate disputes had also been a part of his soul history during the
Trojan War. The reading suggests that, in spite of Homer's account, for a
time the two opposing countries eventually found the means to live in
peace. It also suggests that records of his experiences from that incarnation were still in existence at the time the reading was given (1930):

In the one before this we find in that land known as the Trojan
land. The entity then among those that counseled with Hector and
with Achilles' forces, being a mediator *between* those foes of old,
and bringing much to bear *on* the various forces that gradually
drew the peoples together later in the experiences of that land. In
the name Ashtubol. *Again* the counsel of the entity may be found
as records among those who wrote of the period, *called* that only
in the minds; yet *real* in its actuality. In the influence felt, is that

> halting between opinions of those that would act as the lording
> over others, or as the recognized leaders as varying with the abili-
> ties of self. Establish self rather as one that may be the leader in
> fact.                                                                    5-2

The same year that the attorney received his reading, a fifty–three–
year–old philosophy professor was told that he had supervised some of
the commanders of the Trojan army, and had also served in a mediation
capacity between Greece and Troy:

> In the one, then, before this, we find in that period known as the
> Trojan. The entity then among those people in the land *not* of the
> *warrior* nature, yet ruling many of those that acted in that capac-
> ity, and the mediator between those forces as eventually rose *in*
> the rebellion; becoming, then, that one that acted in the capacity
> of the peacemaker between the forces under Achilles and of Hec-
> tor. In the name Phien. In the innate influences as are seen in the
> experiences of the entity in the present: Many of those things, les-
> sons, elements, taught—as of the nature that were as mythologi-
> cal, to the entity become as *real* as the histories of the entity's own
> land, peoples, or present surroundings. In the influences as this
> brings to the entity: Those of the abilities to judge from the point
> where others differ, by bringing the *correlated* influences *in* each,
> as to an active premise *from* which each, or groups, may reason.
> Then, the entity would have been an excellent politician, or a
> reasoner, or judge.                                                      957-1

In the story of the *Iliad*, Athena managed to break the truce by causing the Trojan warrior Pandaros to wound Menelaus with an arrow.
However, because her sympathies were with the Greeks, she kept the
Greek warrior alive by preventing the arrow from striking a mortal
wound. As a result of this act of aggression, the war began anew and
large numbers of casualties occurred on both sides: "It was a day when
many Trojans and Achaeans [Greeks] bit the dust and were stretched
out side by side." (Rieu, pg. 91)

The battle continued and both armies had their share of victories. However, Athena was not happy with the apparent equality between the two forces. Once again the goddess intervened; this time she inspired the Greek warrior Diomedes with great skill and bravery. Immediately, Diomedes became extremely powerful. He drove the Trojans back and killed many of them in the process, including Pandaros, who had wounded Menelaus. He also wounded Aeneas, the son of Aphrodite. When Aphrodite came to save her son, however, she was wounded in her hand by Diomedes, causing her to return to Olympus where Zeus ordered her to stay off the battlefield. In the end, it was the Greek god Apollo who finally whisked Aeneas to safety.

In order to assist the Trojans, Ares, the god of war, came to the aid of Hector and helped the warrior inspire his forces. Because of the god's intervention and assistance the Greeks were forced to withdraw in the direction of their camp.

Needless to say, neither Hera nor Athena were pleased with the turn of events. The two goddesses gave strength to the Greeks, and Athena caused Diomedes to wound the god Ares with a spear to the stomach, causing Ares to return to Olympus as well. For a time, the battle continued without a god or goddess fighting on either side. The Trojans and Greeks were left to carry out the struggle on their own, using bronze spears, javelins, and arrows.

As the battle raged on, Menelaus captured the Trojan Adrestus, who begged to be ransomed from his father rather than be killed. Menelaus considered the request; however, Agamemnon saw his brother's moment of kindness and shouted that the Trojans would not give him such courtesy. The commander-in-chief demanded that death was the only proper course of action: "The whole people must be wiped out of existence, and none left to think of them and shed a tear." (Rieu, pg. 118) With that, the Trojan was killed with Agamemnon's spear. In the midst of the bloodshed, two combatants, Diomedes and Glaukos, put down their weapons when they discovered that their ancestors had been friends. Their act of reconciliation demonstrated that peace between the two countries was possible; however, the war continued.

With the passage of time it appeared as though the Greeks might be gaining the upper hand. Worried that the Trojans were on the verge of losing, Hector returned to Troy and asked his mother to give offerings to the goddess Athena, winning her favor in the process so that she might assist them. Although his mother did as he requested, Athena refused the offerings and maintained her allegiance to Greece.

While at home, Hector discovered Paris and Helen together in Paris' bedroom. Disgusted, Hector rebuked his younger brother for avoiding the combat. Shamed by his brother, Paris admitted his disgrace and promised to rejoin the battle. While Hector was in the room, Helen made a halfhearted pass at him. She claimed that Hector was a better man than his brother; Hector declined the proposition and departed in order to visit his own wife, Andromache, and their baby son, Astyanax.

While they were together, Hector's wife begged him to stay with the rationale that so many members of her family had already been killed by the war. As much as he wanted to remain, Hector declared that he had no other choice. He said that even though Troy was destined to fall, his duty and honor forced him to return to the battlefield.

In both legend and Homer, Hector is portrayed as a man of honor, of love, and of duty. In his farewell to Andromache and his son, as it is portrayed in the *Iliad*—knowing in all likelihood that he would never see the two again—he prayed to Zeus and tried to comfort his wife's tears:

> "O Zeus and all immortals, may this child, my son, become like me a prince among the Trojans. Let him be strong and brave and rule in power at Ilion; then someday men will say 'This fellow is far better than his father!' seeing him home from war, and in his arms the bloodstained gear of some tall warrior slain—making his mother proud."
>
> After this prayer, into his dear wife's arms he gave the baby, whom on her fragrant breast she held and cherished, laughing through her tears. Hektor [Hector] pitied her now. Caressing her, he said:
>
> "Unquiet soul, do not be too distressed by thoughts of me. You know no man dispatches me into the undergloom against my fate; no mortal either can escape his fate, coward or brave man, once

he [is alive]. Go home, attend to your own handiwork at loom and
spindle, and command the maids to busy themselves, too. As for
the war, that is for men, all who were born at Ilion, to put their
minds on—most of all for me." (Fitzgerald, *Iliad*, Book Two, lines
553-574)

Contrary to the mythic account of Hector's nobleness, kindness,
honor, and loyalty, the Edgar Cayce information provides quite a different portrayal of the Trojan prince. In fact, the readings suggest that
Hector was known as "the usurper" and "the one without heart" (2886-
1), implying that he had stolen the throne and had become a tyrant. As
will be discussed later, the Cayce information contends that the real
Hector was so hated by his people that a number of Trojans allied themselves with the Greeks, hoping that the Greek hero Achilles would lib-
erate them from their oppressive and despotic ruler. Apparently, even
the Trojans knew Achilles' fame as a noble hero. In fact, the readings
suggest that Achilles was truly loved by the masses and known for being a champion of "freedom to the common peoples." (900-38)

In Homer's account of the story, however, after Hector departed from
his family, he rejoined the battle along with his brother Paris.

After the return of both princes, the Trojan army proved so mighty
that Athena feared that all of Greece would be defeated. In order to
provide both armies with a break, she and Apollo arranged to have
Hector challenge the Greek Ajax in a duel meant to settle the conflict.
The opposing warriors came together in hand–to–hand combat, while
the rest of the armies on both sides simply watched and waited.

Hector and Ajax undertook a long, arduous duel, but as it grew dark
it became apparent that neither side had proved victorious. Both men
were considered valiant, a tie was declared, and another truce was called.
The truce provided each army with the opportunity to bury their dead,
because the Greeks believed that improper burial would force a body
to wander for eternity, unable to find rest. While there was a lapse in
combat, the Greeks strengthened their position by building a wall and a
moat around their encampment.

During the evening, a Trojan nobleman, Antenor, suggested that

Helen and her property be returned immediately to Menelaus in order to stop the war. Unfortunately, Paris refused to return Helen but offered instead to return the property he had stolen, as well as some additional money, as a means of settling the conflict.

Meanwhile, Zeus called a council on Olympus and stated that he was about to bring an end to the Trojan War once and for all. He threatened punishment to any god or goddess who interfered with this plan. Nonetheless, in spite of Zeus' pronouncement, Athena asked her father if she could return to the battlefield simply to advise the Greeks; Zeus agreed.

As war continued, Hector and his forces eventually inflicted a tremendous defeat on the Greek army. In fact, the Greeks were so badly beaten and experienced so many casualties that even King Agamemnon was brought to tears and for a time considered retreating home. Others, however, convinced him of their duty to remain in the battle. In order to reinspire the troops, Diomedes stepped forward and gave the Greek forces a rousing speech, promising that victory was inevitable and that Troy was destined to fall.

The wise old Greek warrior Nestor told Agamemnon that he really needed to reconcile with Achilles if he hoped to rally the troops. Agamemnon finally agreed to put an end to the argument. He sent a message to Achilles via Odysseus and Ajax and offered nearly unimaginable rewards: seven tripods, ten talents of gold, twenty cauldrons of copper, twelve race horses, seven women skilled in craftsmanship, twenty Trojan women after the sack of Troy, seven cities, the choice of one of Agamemnon's daughters as bride, and even Briseis herself if the warrior would return to combat. Still, Achilles declined. Again, the king's messengers beseeched the warrior to reconsider: "Conquer your pride, Achilles. You have no right to be so stubborn. [Even] The very gods, for all their greater excellence and majesty and power, are capable of being swayed." (Rieu, pg. 174)

Still, Achilles refused. In spite of the pleas, above all else Achilles desired revenge against Agamemnon. Finally, Odysseus returned to the chief king and said, "Your majesty, the man has no intention of relenting." (Rieu, pg. 179) For that reason, Diomedes told the Greeks that it was senseless to try to change Achilles mind; the Greeks were encouraged to defend their ships against the Trojans.

Seeking information in order to win the war, Agamemnon and Nestor requested that spies be sent to discover the Trojan plans. Both Odysseus and Diomedes accepted the assignment and traveled toward the Trojan camp. On route, they captured Dolon, a Trojan spy who had been sent as a spy to the Greek camp. The Greeks lied to their captive, offering Dolon his life in exchange for information about Hector and the Trojan army. Although Dolon provided the information, he was killed by Diomedes nonetheless.

Perhaps confirming the fact that some of the Greek warriors were not always honorable in their activities, in 1937, a forty–one–year–old house–wife and clothier was told that she had been associated with the Greeks and some of the warriors in positions of leadership. According to the Cayce information, from that experience she had learned to distrust those in leadership positions, since she had apparently witnessed some of the Greek leaders take part in all kinds of depravity and cruel behav–ior:

> There the entity was closely associated with some of the leaders, especially of Achilles' group; for the entity then was nigh unto those activities that made for the *purposes* of the activities during that sojourn.
>
> Hence we find in the present, from that experience as Sujon, there are the doubts of those in authority; yea, for the wild experi–ences in the mental and social activities sought at times—and yet questioning them all.
>
> Yet from that experience also we find again the urge toward things, rather than people. For in the latter portion of that experi–ence the entity sought activities in selling, in the barter of things created by hand, or such things were sought to be a part of the entity's experience.                                    1082-3

According to the mythic account, as fighting continued, Agamemnon led a Greek onslaught against the Trojans. Although he seemed victori–ous for a time, many of the Greek leaders were eventually wounded and the Trojans regained all of the ground they had previously lost. Finally, after Agamemnon, Diomedes, Nestor, and Odysseus had all been wounded, Achilles sent his fellow soldier and best friend Patroklos back to the Greek encampment in order to discover whether the Greeks were truly on the verge of defeat.

When Patroklos reached the army, Nestor explained that their situation was dire. He suggested that short of Achilles returning to the battle-front it would be helpful for Patroklos himself to ride into battle wearing Achilles' armor. Nestor became convinced that the ploy would strike fear into the hearts of the Trojans, as well as inspire and provide renewed hope for the Greek forces.

After his excursion, Patroklos returned to Achilles in great distress. The warrior seemed so affected by what he had seen that Achilles told him that he had the appearance of a little girl walking next to her mother and crying because she wanted to be picked up. Patroklos replied that things were indeed ominous for the Greeks and suggested that Achilles himself might be responsible for what followed:

> **The army is indeed in terrible distress. All of our former champi-ons are lying by their ships, wounded by arrows or spears. The mighty Diomedes son of Tydeus has been hit; Odysseus the great spearman has been wounded; so has Agamemnon; and Eurpylus too has had an arrow in his thigh. Surgeons are attending them with all the remedies at their command, and while they try to heal their wounds, you, Achilles, remain intractable . . . What will fu-ture generations have to thank you for . . . ? (Rieu, pgs. 292-293)**

In spite of Patroklos' best efforts, Achilles refused to return to the battlefield. He remained angry and hurt that Agamemnon had taken the woman that he believed was rightfully his. He told Patroklos that there was nothing that could be done to make him feel otherwise. As a result, Patroklos requested that he might be allowed to lead Achilles' forces into battle. His request went one step further: "And lend me your own armor to put on my shoulders so that the Trojans may take me for you and break off the battle, which would give our weary troops time to recuperate." (Rieu, pg. 293)

According to the tale, Achilles commanded a fleet of fifty ships, each with fifty warriors, simply waiting idle since the argument between Agamemnon and Achilles had begun. Legend states that as the two men were speaking, they saw that the Trojans had set fire to some of the Greek ships:

> **While they spoke the flames burst forth from one of the ships. Achilles, at the sight, relented so far as to grant Patroclus his request to lead the Myrmidons (for so were Achilles' soldiers called) to the field, and to lend him his armour, that he might thereby strike more terror into the minds of the Trojans. Without delay the soldiers were marshaled, Patroclus put on the radiant armour and mounted the chariot of Achilles, and led forth the men ardent for battle. But before he went, Achilles strictly charged him that he should be content with repelling the foe. "Seek not," said he, "to press the Trojans without me, lest thou add more to the disgrace already mine." (Bulfinch, pg. 203)**

Achilles bid farewell and Patroklos departed with instructions only to save the Greek ships; he was not to chase the Trojans back toward the walled city or else he could be killed.

Dressed in Achilles' armor, Patroklos struck fear into the hearts of the Trojan army. The site of the armor and the belief that Achilles had returned to the battlefield immediately caused the Trojan forces to retreat. Fearful and emotionally defeated, Hector and the Trojans returned to their walled city. Rather than following his mentor's advice, however, Patroklos and his army pursued Hector and the Trojan warriors, killing many of them in the process.

Finally, becoming upset by Patroklos' victory, the god Apollo struck him with such a blow that Patroklos lost his helmet and armor. Taking advantage of the situation, a Trojan soldier pierced Patroklos' back with a javelin. Although Patroklos was gravely wounded and attempted to hide, Hector continued the pursuit and finally drove a javelin into the warrior's stomach. Patroklos fell to the ground and before dying told

Hector that even twenty Hectors could not have defeated him, for it was the gods that overcame him and not the Trojans.

The Trojans continued their assault on the Greeks, who were forced to take refuge behind the wall they had built to reinforce their encampment. Eventually Hector and the Trojans broke through the Greek defenses, causing Zeus to feel confident that they no longer needed his assistance. However when Zeus departed, Poseidon moved to the aid of the Greeks and, disguised as the oracle Kalchas, encouraged the Greeks to fight. After a time, Odysseus and the other Greek leaders reinspired the Greek forces.

While Poseidon assisted the Greeks, Hera seduced her husband and caused him to sleep so that the Greek army might have the opportunity to turn the tide of war. Interestingly enough, demonstrating perhaps that the gods were most loyal only amongst themselves, Aphrodite helped Hera seduce Zeus even though the two were on opposing sides.

Fighting intensified over attempts to claim Patroklos' body—and Achilles armor. In the end, the Greeks retrieved the corpse but legend states that Hector captured the armor and decided to wear it as his own.

Because of his friend's death, Achilles was filled with grief and rage. Although his mother advised him that his fate would be death if he tried to avenge Patroklos, Achilles would not be dissuaded. For that reason, his mother promised to outfit him with a new suit of armor made by Hephaestus (Vulcan), the god of fire. When the armor was completed, he returned to battle and finally made amends with Agamemnon. Both the Greeks and the Trojans then prepared for an escalation of fighting.

While the armies prepared for battle, Zeus called an assembly of the gods and once again gave them permission to enter the conflict. Predictably, Poseidon, Hera, Athena, and Hermes moved to help the Greeks. At the same time, Aphrodite, Apollo, and Ares joined forces with Troy.

Once he had reentered the battle, Achilles began a massive revenge against the Trojans. He appeared unbeatable: "Then Achilles went forth to battle inspired with a rage and a thirst for vengeance that made him irresistible." (Bulfinch, pg. 206) In fear, many Trojan warriors fled before him; however, just before he was about to kill Aeneas, the Trojans' second-in-command, Poseidon, rescued the warrior, because the gods had destined that Aeneas would survive. After the rescue, Achilles continued fighting, inflicting major casualties on the Trojan side.

As the battle intensified even the gods warred with one another: Athena fought Ares and Aphrodite; Hera fought Artemis.

Achilles killed so many warriors that the River Xanthos filled with the bodies of dead Trojans. As a result, the god of the river became so angry with Achilles that the Greek warrior was swept into the waters and nearly drowned. He was only saved through the intercession of Hera—who called upon the god of fire to boil the river into nothingness.

The Trojans fled inside their city, leaving Hector to stand outside the gates. Hector stood ready to meet Achilles in hand-to-hand combat. The Trojan prince's parents begged him to come inside the safety of the city walls, but his sense of duty caused him to remain. Although he was afraid and even considered fleeing, the battle between the two opposing forces finally took place.

Hector asked Achilles to treat his body with respect if he lost but Achilles refused, and the final battle between the two began. Although Hector tried to kill Achilles with a spear, the Greek warrior's armor proved invulnerable. Eventually, Achilles lunged forward and stabbed Hector a fatal blow to the throat. As Hector died, he asked that his body be returned to his people for a proper burial. Again, Achilles refused. During his last moments of life, Hector reminded the Greek that Achilles himself was destined to die during the war.

After Hector's death, Achilles stripped the Trojan prince of his armor. He was so angry over the death of Patroklos that he tied the naked corpse to his chariot and disrespectfully dragged the body back to the Greek camp:

> The next thing that Achilles did was to subject the fallen prince to shameful outrage. He slit the tendons at the back of both his feet from heel to ankle, inserted leather straps, and made them fast to the chariot, leaving the head to drag. Then he lifted the famous armor into his car, got in himself, and with a touch of his whip

started the horses, who flew off with a will. Dragged behind him, Hector raised a cloud of dust, his black locks streamed on either side, and dust fell thick upon his head, so comely once, which Zeus now let his enemies defile on his own native soil.

Thus Hector's head was tumbled in the dust. When his mother saw what they were doing to her son, she tore her hair, and plucking the bright veil from her head cast it away with a loud and bitter cry. His father groaned in anguish, the people round them took up the cry of grief, and the whole city gave itself up to despair. (Rieu, pgs. 407-408)

In an amazing dream experience that occurred during the early morning hours of September 19, 1933, Edgar Cayce seemed to be an eyewitness to this very same scene, recounted by Homer, from more than three thousand years earlier. In Cayce's experience, however, Hector was still just barely alive as Achilles dragged him behind the chariot. The dream began with Cayce seeing himself as one of the Trojan guards and then witnessing the final portion of the battle between these two legendary warriors:

I wore a garment that would be called something of a toga today. My trousers were composed of a cloth wrapped around me, gathered and pinned in the middle between my legs. Then another square piece of cloth with a hole for my head dropped over my shoulders. I made armholes in this piece, so that my arms could come through and not have to throw the garment out of the way; which method was afterward adopted by most of the army (or the people, for I didn't recognize them as an army). I saw the battle between Hector and Achilles, recognizing these two as the individuals I now know as [5717] and [900]. They were both beautiful of countenance. Both had matted black ringlets on their heads, which reminded me of Medusa. The hair seemed to be their strength. I noticed that Achilles was very hairy, while Hector only had hair on his neck—which was a different color from the hair on his head. I saw Hector dragged through the gate which I was guarding, into a large arena; and was dragged around the arena several times. Although he was losing, and had lost, quite a bit of blood—leaving the ground and stones bloody as he was dragged along, I noticed that he hadn't wholly lost consciousness. Eventually, the horses—in turning very swiftly, with Achilles driving—caused Hector's head to be dashed against the pillar or the gate near me, and his brains ran out. Before he had even lost the life, or the quiver of the muscles and nerves, I saw the carrion birds eat the great portions of his brain. 294-161

On another occasion in 1929, Edgar Cayce told a forty-year-old manufacturer that he had been the chariot driver for Achilles as the body of Hector was dragged through the city:

In the one before this we find in that period when there were wars in the land called or known as the Trojan period. The entity then among those that assisted Achilles in the deliverance of the people, and the *driver* when Hector was dragged about the city. In the name Ilhouead. The entity lost through the greater portion of this experience, gaining only in the end when peace and quiet was sought in old age, and the influences are those of the right for Right's sake, and the actions toward those that would oppress become as canker to the inmost man. 5540-5

In Homer's account, immediately after the death of Hector the ghost of Patroklos came to Achilles in a dream and asked for a proper funeral so that he could enter death in peace. The next day a large funeral pyre was erected and the body of Patroklos was burned. What bones survived the flames were set aside to be placed with those of Achilles after the warrior's own death.

Every day for nine days after the funeral ceremony, Achilles dragged the naked body of Hector with his chariot around Patroklos' burial mound. Due to the intervention of the gods, Hector's body did not deteriorate. Finally, Zeus held a meeting of the immortals on Olympus and told Thetis that she needed to tell Achilles to return Hector's body to his father.

Meanwhile, Hector's grief–stricken father, King Priam, went to Achilles and begged for the return of his son's body. Overcome by the father's emotion, Achilles relented and the body was returned to the king.

Priam took his son back to the palace and both he and Hecuba were overcome with sadness by their son's death. Greek mythology states that even Helen was deeply affected by what had happened to Hector:

> Hékabê [Hecuba] sobbed again and the wails redoubled. Then it was Helen's turn to make lament:
>
> "Dear Hektor [Hector], dearest brother to me by far! My husband is Aléxandros [another name for Paris], who brought me here to Troy—God that I might have died sooner! This is the twentieth year since I left home, and left my fatherland. But never did I have an evil word or gesture from you. No—and when some other brother-in-law or sister would revile me, or if my mother-in-law spoke to me bitterly—but Priam never did, being as mild as my own father—you would bring her round with your kind heart and gentle speech. Therefore I weep for you and for myself as well, given this fate, this grief. In all wide Troy no one is left who will befriend me, none; they all shudder at me."
>
> Helen wept, and a moan came from the people hearing her.
> (Fitzgerald, *Iliad*, Book Twenty-Four, lines 910-928)

Hector was cremated and his remains were placed in a golden urn and buried in a place of honor. Afterwards, the Trojans held a great funeral banquet in the palace. From that day on, Hector was remembered as a Trojan hero and a "tamer of horses." (Fitzgerald, *Iliad*, Book Twenty-Four, line 961)

The story of the *Iliad* ends with the death of Hector and the funeral banquet in his father's palace.

# 4

# THE TROJAN MYTH IN LEGEND, THE *ODYSSEY*, AND THE *AENEID*

**K**eeping in mind that the Trojan myth was well known among the ancient Greeks and discussed by a variety of sources, Greek mythology explores many aspects of the Trojan tale that are not contained in either Homer or Virgil. For example, although there had been a brief truce between the two nations after Hector's death, legend suggests that fighting resumed between the Greeks and the Trojans when Penthesilea, queen of the Amazons, came to assist the Trojans in their plight. Although she was a mighty warrior, she succumbed in hand–to–hand combat soon after encountering Achilles. (Prince Memnon of Ethiopia came to help the Trojans as an ally as well but he met the same fate as the Amazon queen.)

Interestingly enough, according to Edgar Cayce during this

period in history a number of women had apparently served the city as defenders and warriors. In fact, on two occasions twentieth century women were told that they had been among Troy's female defenses. The first individual was a forty-four-year-old housewife and the second was a thirty-three-year-old social worker. Brief excerpts from each of their readings follow:

> In the experience before this we find in that land known as the Trojan. The entity then in the same sex, yet in the warrior that assisted in the keeping of the gate through which those passed who went to do battle in the field, and especially in the defense of the city. The entity then in the name Milio. In this experience the entity gained through the greater portion of the experience, becoming one who gave much *to* the peoples in an *understanding* manner when contacting those who brought that peace between the armies of that land.                                    2750-1

> In the one before this we find in the land known as the Trojan. The entity then among those that were of the peoples that besought to prevent the entering into the city, and the entity—while in the same sex—defended with self, in bodily form, those that invaded same. Many were the varied conditions as were encountered by the entity during that experience. Many were the conditions that brought for disagreements, misunderstandings, discontent. These often arise in the entity's present experience, through those that *surround* the entity in *closer* relationships. In the name Muriel.
> 6-2

The Edgar Cayce readings suggest that the involvement of various allies may have been due to the fact that the war between the two countries had spread for a time beyond the shores of Troy. For example, in 1935 a twenty-five-year-old government clerk was told that he had taken part in the conflict when it had broken out on the isles of Crete:

> Before that we find the entity was in that land and period which

has often been questioned as to whether it was fact or fiction, in what is described as the Trojan period, when those wars were in the isles of Crete, in the Grecian activity and in the Roman lands—that later became such.

The entity was among those forces and associated with Achilles' activities, in those periods when those men—as men—fought in combat of personal activity for the satisfying of many groups and many nations and many peoples. And during those periods when these were carried on, the entity was then a soldier and a leader among those peoples. And as the entity has read these, or does read these, they will become almost a portion of self in causes, in purposes; for they become as visions to the inmost experience of the entity.

In the name Sheulen (if it were termed in the Arabic characters in the present), the entity in that experience gained and lost; gained during those periods when as the unit the entity aided in establishing a cause, a service for a peoples, though represented by the ideal of an individual; yet when these were turned rather to the indulgences of self and the aggrandizement of personal motives they brought those things that have builded in the present the little hurts that come from slights, from the inabilities to wholly forgive a slight, to wholly forgive or to forget harmful experiences; especially if they bespeak of the character that they are of the motivative force of the entity's activities, rather than the material things. For those pertaining to material things are soon forgotten, yet those to the character of self are as arising and arousing something within that will not lie still.          820-1

On another occasion in 1930, a thirty-two-year-old radio wholesale manager was told that during the Trojan period he had served as an emissary between one-time allies:

In the one before this we find in that land now known as the Grecian. The entity then in that period known as the Trojan, though often called of a mythological nature this *reality* to the entity, and in that experience the entity gained much of that ability to meet circumstances, conditions, relations, that are often hard to be understood by others; yet to the body they become as stepping stones for the successes as may be brought, whether of the mental or of the physical, or of the financial nature. In that period the entity served in the rule of those who defended the city, yet sent as the emissary or the messenger for those in the eastern coast. In the name Odessa. In that experience the entity gained and lost. Gained through the abilities to serve others. Lost in being put into power and aggrandizing of selfish interests brought detrimental influences in the life and the experience during that experience.

2738-1

Greek legend also states that after the fighting resumed, Achilles became involved in a battle that took place just beyond the gates of the Trojan city. During the combat he apparently caught sight of Polyxena, one of the daughters of King Priam and Queen Hecuba. The Greek warrior was so overwhelmed by the girl's beauty that he immediately proposed to Priam that he and Polyxena should be married as soon as peace between Greece and Troy could be established. Unfortunately, it was his infatuation with Polyxena that indirectly led to his downfall:

The betrothal ceremony was held without the city gates; and Achilles was just about to part from his blushing betrothed when Paris, ever treacherous, stole behind him and shot a poisoned arrow into his vulnerable heel, thus slaying the hero who had caused so many brave warriors to bite the dust. (Guerber, pg. 330)

Greek mythology has two versions of what happened to Polyxena after the death of her beloved. In one account, she was so inconsolable that she committed suicide on his tomb. According to another version, the Greeks sacrificed Polyxena on Achilles' tomb at the end of the Trojan War as an offering to the gods.

Legend also states that it had been the god Apollo who had expertly guided the poison arrow, assuring that it would find the fatal mark in

Achilles' heel. After the death of Achilles, the Greeks retrieved the body of their slain hero, and an argument broke out between Odysseus and Ajax regarding who had rightful claim to Achilles' armor. When it was finally awarded to Odysseus, Ajax became insanely furious and threatened to kill some of the Greek warriors in revenge. Later, Ajax, considering his actions to be dishonorable, committed suicide.

With the deaths of Achilles and Ajax, two of Greece's greatest warriors, the Greeks became anxious about taking Troy once and for all. They consulted an oracle to learn how Troy might be defeated. Some legends suggest that the oracle was the Greek seer Kalchas; others contend that it was Helenus, a Trojan prophet and seer, who had been kidnapped and happened to be one of Hector's younger brothers. In any event, the oracle informed them that Troy could never be taken without the poisoned arrows of Hercules. Unfortunately, Hercules was dead, and his bow and arrows were in the possession of Philoctetes, a Greek warrior whom the Greek's had unceremoniously abandoned on an island ten years earlier while on their journey to the Trojan War. Philoctetes' offense had simply been that he had wounded himself in the foot with one of the arrows (one legend states that he had actually been bitten by a snake), but the horrible stench put off from his decaying flesh was so offensive that none of the other Greeks could stomach being around him.

Interestingly enough, this legendary story sounds much like the symptoms of acute gangrene—a decaying of the flesh that results in a putrid-smelling gaseous discharge. A remarkable anecdote in this regard is that Edgar Cayce pinpointed the actual death of Achilles as apparently being due to a bacterially infected arrow that resulted in the formation of gangrene in his heel and eventually blood poisoning: "The entity then departed the life in personal combat, wounded in the heel, from which gangrene set in in body and became blood poison to the system." (900–63)

Because of the oracle's advice, Philoctetes was sent for and eventually found. By this time a son of the god Asclepius, the Greek god of healing, had healed him so that his foot no longer reeked. In spite of his anger at being stranded for ten years, he agreed to assist the army.

Philoctetes arrived with the bow and arrows of Hercules, and Paris became the first victim of their deadly poison.

Another legend suggests that Troy could not be taken as long as a
statue of Athena, called the Palladium, remained in her temple at Troy.
Odysseus and Diomedes entered the city in disguise and managed to
steal the statue, but still Troy did not fall.

It was the gods themselves who finally decided that ten years of war
was long enough. The time had come to bring it to an end, so Athena
sent Odysseus the idea for the Trojan horse. According to legend, a
Greek named Epeios was the actual architect of the wooden horse,
which Odysseus filled with fighters and took into the city. Although the
Trojan horse is briefly mentioned in Homer's *Odyssey*, for the most part
the epic has little to do with the actual events of the Trojan War.

During the years he gave readings, Edgar Cayce told several individuals that they had been involved in the construction of the Trojan
horse; two were Greeks and one was a Trojan. According to the readings, the architect for the horse was a Greek by the name of Cajhalon,
not Epeios. During the course of his life reading, this thirty-five-year-
old construction engineer was told that he had been the horse's chief
builder and had died during the siege of the city. The reading suggests
that the invading Greek warriors set the city (and perhaps even the
Trojan horse) aflame as part of their battle strategy:

> In the one before this we find in the days of the Trojan, and the
> forces of that country in Greece. The entity then in that of
> Cajhalon, was the builder and the actual worker on the Horse led
> or pushed into the surrounding foe, that the city might be cap-
> tured. The entity then of beautiful figure and stature, and held as
> one of noble descent and of special gifts from the gods. The entity
> losing its life, however, at that period, in the siege as was made
> following this burning. In the death, or birth at that time (for they
> are one and the same), the entity found the development for self.
> 470-2

In 1934, a twenty-year-old man was told that he had also been among the Greeks who had helped plan the method by which the Greeks could enter the city of Troy; the ruse had included the use of the Trojan horse:

> **Before that we find the entity was in the Grecian or Trojan activities when there were the rebellions of those peoples, and the attempt for the gathering together of those to *storm* the city.**
>
> **The entity then was among those who prepared the ways and means for entering into the city.**
>
> **Then, in the present there is the interest that may be aroused—from reading of the horse that was rolled in at the gate—in activities pertaining to not exactly undermining and taking advantage of others, but the matching wits one with another; which is the activity innately and manifested in the entity's experience. Hence, the abilities to work out problems that require the activities in these directions are things that may be applied in the experience of the entity. And again we may find the same activities in the associations as to communications in various relationships with individuals, groups, and those that make for the better or the broader developments. The name then was Ulan.          568-1**

While viewing this period in history, Edgar Cayce also perceived the use of mechanical weaponry in addition to the Trojan horse. In all likelihood, the weapons available to the Greeks and Trojans included battle-axes, arrows, daggers, the horse and chariot, and perhaps even rudimentary projectile weapons. In 1942, Cayce told a forty-five-year-old bowling alley manager that during the Trojan War he had been skilled at making weapons. It was a skill that apparently remained with him at a soul level and caused him to imagine "ingenious things for defense" during World War II:

> **Before that the entity was in the Trojan War period, when there were those mechanical applications made to the weapons of defense as well as weapons of destruction.**
>
> **There the entity, in the name Rekulus, was active in such expe-**

riences as to bring the present desires for making ingenious things for defense. And these have been a part of the entity's experience oft in its activity, and in its associations with various influences.

The entity gained materially through those experiences, yet because there were those able even to use the entity's ideas to improve on same there came discouragements and doubts as to the abilities of others to attain or acquire or apply other than by building on the offices or activities of others.

These brought the anxieties and hates, and these account for the likes and dislikes that are so severe in the entity's experience in its associations with individuals.                    2813-1

Finally, in 1930, a thirty-six-year-old shirt manufacturer was informed that he had been among those Trojans who sympathized with Achilles and had resented the rule of Hector. For that reason, he had been one of those who had assisted the invading army, going so far as to help create some of the mechanical movements of the legendary horse:

In the one before this we find in that period known as the Trojan. The entity then of those that aided in the defense of the city, and especially under the influence of Achilles during that period. Not so much the soldier, as one preparing the way for those who would wage war, and making of weapons during portion of the period, and among those who made for the mechanical arrangements of the horse and its workings, in the latter portion. In the name Parsia. In the experience the entity gained much during the early portion, losing in the latter through that of the *feeling builded* as *resentment to* those in power; yet innate there is felt in the present those of too much honor due those who have succeeded in position or power, or in money, or in fame. Rather does the entity see that position, than as to how, why, or when same was acquired. 2856-1

Greek mythology states that Odysseus had been away from home for twenty years, just as had been prophesied by an oracle. Homer's

*Odyssey* essentially covers a period of six weeks during the last ten years of "the wanderings of Odysseus." Two nights of that period are taken up simply for Odysseus to narrate his adventures to an eager audience—adventures that began when the hero attempted to return to Ithaca after the war but was prevented from doing so through the intervention of one of the immortals at Olympus. Ironically, legend tells how it was Athena herself—Odysseus' strongest supporter—who was responsible for delaying the hero's homecoming. Apparently, after the war one of the Greek warriors either raped or attempted to rape Cassandra in Athena's temple. Because the man went unpunished, Athena caused the entire army to be blown off course, resulting in the start of Odysseus' long journey. According to the tale, as the years passed Odysseus ended up being the only Greek warrior who had survived the war but had failed to return home.

Odysseus' adventures included a variety of lands and people that imprisoned him or attempted to entrap him with desire. He encountered the Lotus-eaters, whose food caused individuals to lose all thoughts of their home and caused them to wish to remain in their country. He came to the home of Polyphemus, the Cyclops and a son of Poseidon, whom he blinded. His wanderings included a land of cannibals; an encounter with a witch; and even an experience with the dead in Hades. Finally, the goddess Calypso imprisoned him and held him as her lover-captive for seven years.

Meanwhile, back at his home on Ithaca, a line of suitors had continuously courted his wife Penelope—as many believed that King Odysseus was dead and they hoped that his throne and his wife might become theirs. In the intervening years, Odysseus' son Telemachus had also come of age.

With the passage of time, Athena finally decided to come to Odysseus' aid. Obtaining the permission of Zeus, the goddess traveled to Ithaca and, while in disguise, she encouraged Telemachus to seek word of his father by telling him that Odysseus was not dead, only "detained." She suggested that the young man track down his father by first tracking down Odysseus' fellow warriors: Nestor in Pylos and Menelaus in Sparta. Athena also encouraged Telemachus to throw all of Penelope's suitors off of the estate, for even after twenty years, Penelope still mourned her husband.

Although intrigued by the possibility of finding Odysseus, Telemachus had a difficult time believing at first that his father was still alive. Upon awakening the next morning, however, Telemachus called an assembly of everyone on the estate. The surprise gathering caused some to believe that Odysseus' return was about to be announced, but instead Telemachus stated that two "troubles" had befallen his household. The first was that his father remained lost and the second was that a long line of suitors had been pestering his mother to get married against her will:

> My distinguished father is lost, who ruled among you once, mild as a father, and there is now this greater evil still: my home and all I have are being ruined. Mother wanted no suitors, but like a pack they came . . . these men spend their days around our hose, killing our beeves [oxen/cattle] and sheep and fatted goats, carousing, soaking up our good dark wine, not caring what they do. They squander everything. (Fitzgerald, *Odyssey*, Book Two, lines 49-54, 59-62)

After he announced that the suitors were eating him and his mother out of house and home, many of those in attendance were moved to pity; however, Antinous, one of Penelope's most determined suitors, instead placed the blame on Telemachus' own mother. He suggested that Penelope had toyed with their emotions, played them against one another, and essentially encouraged them to pursue her. In fact, she had apparently promised several of them that she would marry as soon as she had finished weaving a burial shroud for Odysseus' elderly father, Laertes. Her suitors had eventually discovered, however, that she had worked on the shroud daily for three years and then unstitched her work at night, as a means of never having to fulfill her promise. When her ruse was exposed, she had to complete the shroud.

Because of Penelope's behavior, Antinous suggested that Telemachus had to evict his mother from the estate or at least force her into marrying one of them. Demonstrating his father's wisdom and creating a delay, Telemachus suggested instead that he and a crew go in search of Odysseus. If he found his father dead, he would allow his mother to remarry.

During Telemachus' journey to find news of his father, Nestor, Menelaus, and Helen each have opportunities to describe some of the events of the Trojan War.

When Telemachus and his crew reached Nestor, the old warrior stated that he was not certain what had befallen Odysseus. After the Trojan War, Menelaus and Agamemnon were apparently provoked into fighting one another because of the intervention and influence of Athena. In fact, the argument between the two had caused each of their armies to separate.

Hearing of Telemachus' plan to go in search of his father, Nestor told the young man the story of what had happened to Agamemnon while he had been far from home. Agamemnon had married Clytemnestra, one of Helen's sisters. As Agamemnon had been away for so many years fighting the war, another man named Aigisthos had won over Agamemnon's queen, enabling him to rule Agamemnon's kingdom for seven years as a dictator. Upon Agamemnon's return, both his wife and her lover killed him. Although Agamemnon's son eventually avenged his father's death by having the two of them killed, the tragedy might never have happened had the old king not been so far from home for such a length of time. For that reason, Nestor advised Telemachus not to stay away so long himself. Nonetheless, he encouraged him to proceed to Sparta in search of King Menelaus, who might know more. (It is from the *Odyssey* and other sources that we also learn that Clytemnestra herself became responsible for the murder of Cassandra, who had become Agamemnon's captured concubine after the fall of Troy. In fact, after the war the Greeks had divided the surviving Trojan women amongst themselves as slaves and concubines.)

Following the encouragement of both Athena and Menelaus, the journey took Telemachus and his followers to the mansion of Menelaus, who discussed some of his own memories of the war. After the siege of Troy, Menelaus had reunited with Helen, from whom he had been separated for twenty years. (According to some versions of the legend, upon meeting his unfaithful wife in Priam's palace, Menelaus was about to put a sword through her heart but was stopped by Aphrodite—the goddess who had been responsible for Helen's abduction in the first place.) After their meeting, the two resumed their marriage. Legend suggests that the two had sailed through much of the Mediterranean before finally arriving back at their home in Sparta, where they would live out the remainder of their days. According to legend, the couple would have one daughter named Hermione, who some say married Neoptolemus, the only son of Achilles. (In some legends, Neoptolemus is also called Pyrrhus.)

In spite of the passage of years, Telemachus saw that Helen had remained a beauty: " . . . Helen came out of her scented chamber, a moving grace like Artemis [goddess of hunting and chastity], straight as a shaft of gold." (Fitzgerald, *Odyssey*, Book Four, lines 131–133)

Menelaus told Telemachus that he loved Odysseus more than he had loved any other warrior and that he had been deeply saddened that the boy's father had failed to return home. Helen proceeded to tell the tale of how Odyssey had entered the city of Troy disguised as a beggar in order to spy upon the Trojans, gathering information that had helped the Greek cause:

> Not that I think of naming, far less telling, every feat of that rugged man, Odysseus, but here is something that he dared to do at Troy, where you Akhaians [Greeks] endured the war. He had, first, given himself an outrageous beating and thrown some rags on— like a household slave—then slipped into that city of wide lanes among his enemies. So changed, he looked as never before upon the Akhaian beachhead, but like a beggar, merged in the townspeople; and no one there remarked him. But I knew him—even as he was, I knew him . . . and swore an oath not to give him away as Odysseus to the Trojans, till he got back to camp where the long ships lay. He spoke up then, and told me all about the Akhaians and their plans . . . my heart sang—for I had come round, long before, to dreams of sailing home, and I repented the mad day

### Aphroditê drew me away . . . (Fitzgerald, Odyssey, Book Four, lines 258-269, 272-276, 279-283)

During their meeting, Menelaus also recounted how he, Odysseus, Diomedes, and others had been inside the body of the hollow Trojan horse when Helen had been drawn to the horse by some superhuman power and forced to walk around it. Three times she had encircled the creature, patted its sides and even called out the names of Greek warriors and disguised her voice to appear to be that of their wives. Only the presence of Odysseus had managed to keep one of the men from shouting out and revealing their place of hiding.

The next day Menelaus told Telemachus how he and his army had been stranded on their journey home and had to capture the god Proteus (an assistant to Poseidon) in order to escape. It was from Proteus that Menelaus had learned that Odysseus had become a prisoner on Calypso's island.

As Telemachus journeyed to return home, back in Ithaca Penelope's suitors plotted to have him ambushed and killed. Meanwhile, Odysseus remained Calypso's love prisoner. Finally, Athena pleaded to Zeus that the two needed the help of the gods. As a result, Zeus sent Athena to help Telemachus and sent Hermes to help Odysseus.

After Odysseus had escaped from the isle of Calypso and arrived at the kingdom of Phaeacia, an assembly was called in which the blind minstrel Demodocus sang of the fall of Troy and the efforts of the Greek heroes and warriors to take the city. Although the identity of Odysseus was unknown when the tale began, he was so moved by the song that he began to cry and admitted who he was. He then proceeded to tell of his own wanderings after a final raid at the end of the war, " . . . when we pulled away from death. And this new grief we bore with us to sea: our precious lives we had, but not our friends." (Fitzgerald, *Odyssey*, Book Nine, lines 68–70)

In the end, the *Odyssey* tells two stories: Telemachus' search for his father and the young man's coming of age, as well as the adventures of Odysseus and the heroes eventual return to prove whom he is and to reclaim his wife and throne.

In addition to Greek mythology, legend, and Homer's epics, Virgil's *Aeneid* gives insights into the Greek–Trojan conflict and additional information on some of the characters, the Trojan horse, and the final siege of the city. Written by Virgil over a period of eleven years, only the rough draft was finished when Virgil became severely ill and unexpectedly died in 19 B.C. Although he had left instructions to have the epic destroyed, his friend, the emperor Augustus, refused and instead had two of Virgil's friends prepare the work for publication. Shortly thereafter, the *Aeneid* was published.

Virgil's tale is composed of twelve books, describing the adventures and wanderings of Aeneas after the Trojan War. The purpose of the story was to incorporate legend and myth and to trace the journey of the Trojan Aeneas and some of his followers to their eventual settling in Italy, where they would become the ancestors of the founders of the Rome. Rome traced its roots to the Trojan Myth.

Almost as soon as it was written, the Romans essentially adopted the *Aeneid* as their national epic. The tale was written in Latin rather than Greek and because it was composed for a Roman audience, the gods and goddesses of Homer's epics took on the names of their Roman equivalents, just as Odysseus took on the name Ulysses. In terms of the Trojan War, only the second book relates to the fall of Troy. The remainder of the *Aeneid* deals with the adventures of the surviving Trojans and the wanderings of Aeneas, his romances, his battles, and his ultimate victory over the Latins (natives of Italy), enabling the Trojans and the Latins to live in peace and lay the foundations of what would become the Roman Empire.

The *Aeneid* tells how the surviving remnant of Troy escaped by sea, only to be threatened by the hatred of Juno (Hera). In addition to having been once snubbed by Paris, Juno was angry because it had been predicted that Trojan descendants would eventually rule the known world, even conquering her favorite people of Carthage. Juno believed that by destroying the Trojans, she could effectively change the prophecy, enabling the people of Carthage to rule the world instead. She had also been long upset by the fact that her husband Jupiter (Zeus) had once appointed a handsome young male Trojan by the name of

Ganymede to be the eternal cup–bearer and wine–pourer for the gods on Olympus. Not only was she seemingly jealous of her husband's relationship with the youth but she undoubtedly believed that the honor far surpassed his Trojan birth.

According to legend, after the war Aeneas led a Trojan remnant composed of twenty ships in search of a more hospitable country. After wandering throughout the Mediterranean, they decided to sail from Sicily in the direction of the ancient country of Hesperia, which had come to be called Italy. While at sea during the last portion of their journey, they were forced to battle fierce windstorms that had been sent by Aeolus, the god of the winds, who had been influenced and bribed by Juno. The winds caused much of the small fleet to be separated. The storms were so powerful that they threatened to destroy every ship and kill every Trojan. Finally Neptune (Poseidon) intervened and saved them, not because he was on the side of the Trojans but because he was angry that his kingdom of the sea had been unduly influenced by Aeolus and Juno.

When Venus (Aphrodite) complained about how her son Aeneas was being treated by Juno, Jupiter simply promised that in spite of how things appeared the Trojans would be successful in their quest and that the descendants of Aeneas would found the city of Rome. Jupiter also predicted the eventual birth of individuals such as Romulus and Remus and even Julius, "the Trojan Caesar." (Fitzgerald, *Aeneid*, Book One, line 385)

When Aeneas and his seven remaining ships finally reached the shores of Africa, he and his devoted armor–bearer Achates met a disguised Venus, who told them of Carthage, the nearby kingdom of Queen Dido. Originally from Tyre, Dido and her people had immigrated to the coast after the death of her husband. The queen had purchased a great deal of property from the locals and was in the process of establishing their new home.

Magically hidden from view, Aeneas and Achates entered Carthage where they discovered a wall of paintings that detailed the Trojan War and the siege and destruction of their city. They also witnessed Dido extend her hospitality to the missing Trojan captains, from whom they had been separated, when they also arrived at the kingdom. Because of the queen's benevolence, Aeneas sent for gifts from his ship, asking his son Ascanius to deliver them personally. Because of the intervention of Venus, however, Amor (Cupid) arrived disguised as Ascanius and influenced Dido to begin to fall hopelessly in love with Aeneas.

During a banquet meant to honor the Trojans and provide them with food and drink, Queen Dido asked Aeneas to tell his story: "Come . . . dear guest, and tell us from the beginning the Greek stratagems, the ruin of your town and your sea-faring, as now the seventh summer brings you here from wandering all the lands and all the seas." (Fitzgerald, *Aeneid*, Book One, lines 1027–1037)

To be sure, relating the story of Troy's demise filled Aeneas' heart with sadness but he proceeded to tell the story of how the Greeks had finally been able to take the city after ten years of fighting. According to Aeneas, the Greeks spread the rumor that they were leaving and they built a hollow wooden horse as tall as a hill that appeared to be an offering to the goddess Minerva (Athena), assuring their safe return back home. However, within the belly of the horse the Greeks had hidden a fully armed company of men—nine captains and their accompanying warriors, perhaps as many as fifty warriors in all! Unbeknownst to the Trojans, rather than retreating, the Greek army had instead hidden their fleet on the other side of Tenedos Island.

Roman mythology confirms the fact that it was only after having tried everything else to take the city that the idea for the Trojan horse finally came into being:

> **The Greeks then constructed an immense *wooden horse*, which they gave out was intended as a propitiatory offering to Minerva, but in fact was filled with armed men. The remaining Greeks then betook themselves to their ships and sailed away, as if for a final departure. The Trojans, seeing the encampment broken up and the fleet gone, concluded the enemy to have abandoned the siege. The gates were thrown open, and the whole population issued forth rejoicing at the long-prohibited liberty of passing freely over the scene of the late encampment. The great *horse* was the chief ob-**

> ject of curiosity. All wondered what it could be for. Some recom-
> mended to take it into the city as a trophy; others felt afraid of it.
> (Bulfinch, pg. 212)

When it appeared that the Greeks were gone, the city gates were thrown open and many of the Trojans went out in joy to find the Greek campsites deserted and burned, and the Trojan horse left behind. According to Aeneas, the people marveled at the size of the creature. Some wanted it hauled inside the city gates. Others wanted it thrown into the sea or burned. Someone even suggested that the hollow belly of the horse should be opened and searched, but in the end the crowd simply argued among themselves as to what was to be done.

Finally, a Trojan named Laocoön came forward and warned the others that he feared a ruse: "Have no faith in the horse! Whatever it is, even when Greeks bring gifts I fear them, gifts and all." (Fitzgerald, *Aeneid*, Book Two, lines 68–70) Legend states that Cassandra herself also predicted doom, but none would listen.

Immediately after Laocoön expressed his fears, the Trojans captured a Greek by the name of Sinon. Unbeknownst to the Trojans, Sinon had been purposely left behind by Ulysses (Odysseus) to lie to his captors in order to make the Greek ploy complete. The lie that Sinon told was that he had barely escaped from being used as a human sacrifice because he and Ulysses had become bitter enemies. For that reason he claimed to no longer have an allegiance to the Greeks.

Sinon told his listeners that the goddess Minerva (Athena) had deserted the Greeks because Diomedes and Ulysses had stolen the Palladium from its temple. According to Sinon's story, because the goddess had abandoned them, the Greeks did not believe they could win the war, so they had decided to depart. In order to reach their home shores safely, they chose Sinon to be their human sacrifice, but he escaped. The horse was left to appease the angry goddess, and the Greeks hoped that the Trojans would destroy it, earning the goddess's wrath in return. (Some legends suggest that the horse was actually an offering to Neptune, who is sometimes personified in the image of a horse.)

Unfortunately for the Trojans, Sinon's lies sounded convincing, and they ignored Laocoön's pleas. Since it appeared that Minerva was connected to the horse, the people decided to bring the creature inside the city. However, the horse was too large to fit through the gates. For that reason, a portion of the city's walls had to be removed so that the Trojan horse could be dragged inside.

While the people dragged the horse inside Troy, Laocoön prepared a sacrifice to the gods as a means of protecting them from the deception:

> **Deaf to all warnings and entreaties, they dragged the colossal image into the very heart of their city, tearing down a portion of their ramparts to allow its passage, while Laocoön hastened down to shore to offer sacrifice to the gods. As he stood there by the improvised altar, with one of his sons on either side to assist him in his office, two huge serpents came out of the sea, coiled themselves around him and his sons, and crushed and bit them to death. (Guerber, pg. 333)**

In Virgil's account the Trojan people witnessed the sea snakes (obviously sent by the god Neptune) landing upon the exact spot where Laocoön had stood with his two sons. They took it as an omen to completely ignore Laocoön's advice.

According to Edgar Cayce, rather than the Trojan horse simply being a Greek deception, many Trojans were also involved in the plot that eventually overthrew the city's despotic ruler. Interestingly enough, in Cayce's rendering of the events leading up to the fall of the city, Achilles was still alive after the ruse of the Trojan horse had allowed Greek warriors into the city. In fact, in 1929, a fifty-one-year-old osteopath was told in her reading that she had been an aide to Paris who had helped Achilles enter Troy by calling to her son to open the gates when the time was right:

> **In the one before this we find in that period that has often been called mythological, when in Troy—and the siege of same. The entity then an aide and assistant—yet still in the sex as the woman, but an aide to that one over whom the dispute arose; aid-**

ing particularly when Paris and Hector and Achilles first drew the
lines for the array before the city. The entity then, not as a soldier,
not as a servant. Rather as the aide to that one that brought about
such dissensions; aided Achilles in *entering* the gate, by calling to
the son (and is the son [102] still) to open when called. In the
present we find much of that vim, that application of power. Used
aright, a blessing. Used awrong, a curse. In the name Xenia, and
the entity has often wondered when those letters were put together.
The innate self may gain *much* by the study of the name, even as
written. Many visions, of many fields, of many positions, of many
places, may be brought close to the consciousness by meditation
on *just* a name.                                              101-1

In 1934, an eighteen–year–old student was informed that during the
Trojan period she had been married to one of the gatekeepers. She was
also among those who had conspired against Hector; and, according to
Cayce, her drawings at the time had proved invaluable at enabling
Achilles' warriors to defeat the city's defenses:

> Before that we find the entity was in that land now known as the
> Roman, or rather the Grecian and Roman, during the periods when
> there were what are now known as the Trojan Wars, during the
> activities between those over that entity Helen of Troy.
>
> During those activities the entity then was the companion of
> the assistant keeper of the gate to the city, and during the experi-
> ence the drawings of the entity enabled those that were of the
> besieged to encounter—in part, in the main; though little credit
> was given Garcia in the experience, yet such enabled the armies—
> or the individual activities of those in Achilles' activities—to suc-
> ceed in bringing destruction to Hector's forces. And the entity saw
> those activities.
>
> Hence the abilities in the writing, or to depict by word or by
> drawing, or by the activities in the artistic temperament, arise
> from the associations in that experience.                    259-8

To be sure, in Edgar Cayce's view of this period in history not every Trojan had been involved in Hector's overthrow. During a life reading given in September 1932, a twenty–year–old male was told that he had originally defended the gates against the invading Greeks but after Achilles had overtaken the city, he had apparently switched his allegiance. In time, he eventually gained a position of power, becoming an overbearing authority in his own right:

> In the one before this we find during that period when there were those in the Trojan developments. The entity then was one of those who defended when the gates of the city were broken up. Then, in the name Smoniel, the entity gained and lost. Taking sides rather with that entity who led the people in the destruction of Hector and his people, the entity became *overbearing*—through the power that came into the entity's experience in that period. In the present there will be the need for power and position to be tempered with spiritual and mental judgment.                    1225-2

On a different occasion, another supporter of Hector's reign came in the form of a twenty–five–year–old construction engineer who was told that during this period in history he had apparently been an immigrant to Troy and had defended the city against "those that would destroy their own city," losing his life in the process:

> Before this in the Trojan forces, when the defense of the City was at hand, this body then was that individual who stood in the gate defying those from without, and in that bore the brunt of those that would destroy their own city in which this entity then claimed as the home, you see, though not of that people. The name then we find was Ixnoz, (interpretation) the defense of the fair, the defense of those that would give the forces to the world for developing the future age.                    4121-2

In any event, according to legend when nightfall came and it appeared as though the Greek–Trojan conflict had finally come to an end, a great celebration was held throughout the city. The people drank and feasted well into the evening; apparently, they had no idea that they were on the verge of destruction:

> So feasted they through Troy, and in their midst loud pealed the flutes and pipes: on every hand were song and dance, laughter and cries confused of banqueters beside the meats and wine. They, lifting in their hands the beakers brimmed, recklessly drank, till heavy of brain they grew, till rolled their fluctuant eyes. Now and again some mouth would babble the drunkard's broken words. The household gear, the very roof and walls seemed as they rocked: all things they looked on seemed whirled in wild dance. About their eyes a veil of mist dropped, for the drunkard's sight is dimmed, and the wit dulled, when rise the fumes to the brain: And thus a heavy-headed feaster cried: "for naught the Danaans [Greeks] mustered that great host hither! Fools, they have wrought not their intent, but with hopes unaccomplished from our town like silly boys or women have they fled." So cried a Trojan wit-befogged with wine, fool, nor discerned destruction at the doors. (Way, *Quintus Smyrnaeus,* Book Thirteen, lines 1-20)

That night while the city slept, the Greeks set sail from Tenedos and returned to the Trojan shores. Meanwhile, Sinon set free Ulysses and his men who had remained quiet inside the belly of the Trojan horse. The city would encounter a surprise attack from without and from within. The nine captains left inside the horse dropped a rope from its belly and one at a time climbed down hand over hand to the city below. According to the *Aeneid,* the nine were as follows: Thessandrus, Sthenelus, Ulysses, Acamas, Thoas, Neoptolemus, Machaon, Menelaus, and Epeios. (The warrior Diomedes who had been named in the *Odyssey* as one of those within the belly of the horse is not listed in Virgil's account.) Their first task was to kill the city's sentries and then to let in the rest of the Greek warriors, who would be waiting just outside the gates.

Meanwhile, while Troy was being attacked, the ghost of Hector came to Aeneas in a dream and told him what was befalling the city. The dead warrior told Aeneas that he and a band of Trojans had to leave the city immediately so that they could escape and eventually found a new Troy elsewhere. When Aeneas finally awoke, the city was under siege; the voices of thousands broke the stillness of night.

Once war was underway, many of the Trojans remained at their posts and tried to protect the city from the invading warriors. The following Cayce readings were given for individuals who were among those that attempted to defend the walls and the gates of Troy during the siege. The first reading was given to an eight–year–old boy who had been a musician before being conscripted into the war. The second was given to a thirty–six–year–old furniture salesman, who was told that prior to the war, as a guard at the gate he had gained the ability to communicate with all kinds of people; unfortunately, he had been killed while de-fending the gates:

> In the one before this we find the entity as the soldier, in then the Trojan forces. The entity among those who defended the gate, when these were overcome by those from the outside, and the entity gained and lost during this sojourn. Then in the name Abidouel, and the entity then a man of valor, and in the service brought much condemnation to others through the justice as was meted out by the entity's acts during that period. The urge as is seen in the musical tend or bent comes from this period; for in the early por-tion of life the entity among those who made music before the fair ones of the land in which the entity sojourned, and ever runs the desire to keep close to such conditions. Hence the bugle and the drum mean much to the entity, and—guided aright—this may be-come a crowning glory in the present experience.        5454-3

> In the one, then, before this, we find in that experience during the period known as the Trojan. The entity was among those who de-fended the walls and the gates, and was among those who builded against the entering in of the peoples through that of strategy, losing the life in the defense of same. In the whole of the experi-

ence the entity gained and lost, gaining in the service and in *giv-*
*ing* of self for others. In the present we find those abilities to meet
peoples in every walk of life and to *view* same from the varied
experiences of self, and from the *individual's* experience, making
for the ability as of the *salesman* in *this* experience.        1739-8

In Virgil's *Aeneid,* although Aeneas had his weapons and fought some
of the Greek warriors, it was soon clear that the entire Greek army had
entered the city and any hope of winning the battle was doomed to
failure. For that reason, he disguised himself in the armor of one of the
slain Greeks and rushed to the palace of Priam in order to protect the
aged king. Unfortunately, he arrived just in time to see the Trojan king
murdered by Neoptolemus, Achilles' only son.

According to legend, most of the city was in flames. The entire Greek
army had surrounded Troy—Greek ships could be seen in the harbor as
far as the eye could see. Hector's infant son Astyanax was thrown from
the city walls to his death on the ground below. Cassandra was dragged
from the temple of Minerva and raped. Afterwards, the Greeks took
both Cassandra and Hecuba as prisoners. The people of Troy were
doomed.

During the siege, Aeneas came upon Helen—the cause of the city's
demise—and pondered killing her but was stopped by his mother Venus, who reminded him that even before Helen's presence, the gods
had long decreed that the city would fall: "Catching me by the hand,
she held me back, then with her rose-red mouth reproved me: 'Son,
why let such suffering goad you on to fury past control?'" (Fitzgerald,
*Aeneid,* Book Two, lines 780–782) Instead the goddess urged him to find
his own wife Creusa and his son Ascanius, as both were still alive. She
also enabled him to see what was hidden from view of most mortals—
many of the gods were participating in the fighting and were helping to
destroy the city walls, including Jupiter, Juno, Neptune, and Minerva.

Venus convinced her son to leave the city as quickly as possible. He
hurried home, took his aged father Anchises on his back (at first, the
man was reluctant to leave), grabbed his son Ascanius by the hand and
told his wife Creusa to follow. His servants were also informed where to

meet. When he arrived at the meeting place, he had his father and his son by his side and many of his servants. However, when he turned he could see that his wife was no longer there. Hurriedly he retraced his steps to his house where he was met by Creusa's ghost, who assured him that he needed to proceed to the banks of the Tiber and that once there he would find a beautiful young bride who would comfort him for his loss. Full of sadness, he returned to the meeting place just beyond the city walls and found that another group of Trojans had joined his household, all awaiting his leadership.

When the group had gathered, Aeneas led them all into the hills surrounding Mount Ida, from where the surviving Trojans saw their entire city on fire. In fact, legend suggests that the destruction was so complete that by daybreak all of the people of Troy were either dead or in bondage.

Because the people of Troy had been so thoroughly annihilated, even the gods were offended. For that reason, according to Greek mythology most of the Greek warrior–kings received "the wrath of the gods" (Guerber, pg. 337) for their involvement in the siege. In fact, much of the Greek fleet was destroyed by storms while homeward bound; many of the leaders would die before ever returning and some like Agamemnon would be killed; Odysseus was forced to wander for years.

As for the surviving Trojans, however, in time, Aeneas led his followers to the open sea. They journeyed first to Thrace to establish their new city, but the very ground seemed cursed with the bodies of slain Trojans from an earlier expedition. When Aeneas broke the branch off a bush, the body of Polydore, a young Trojan prince who had long been dead, called out from the ground: "Spare me, Aeneas; I am your kinsman, Polydore, here murdered with many arrows, from which a bush has grown, nourished with my blood." (Bulfinch, pg. 238) For that reason, the group of surviving Trojans continued on their journey.

They sailed to Delos where the oracle of Apollo encouraged them to continue the journey to their true ancestral home, which Aeneas' father Anchises interpreted to mean Crete. As if to confirm this course of the Trojan journey, in 1925 Edgar Cayce informed a seventeen–year–old girl that in a former incarnation she had been a Greek woman, captured by the Trojans, who had been taken to Crete:

> In the one before this we find in the Grecian country when the
> Trojan Wars were then in that country, and the entity then in that
> of Aphori and was one of those taken prisoner by the Trojans and
> carried to the isle of Crete, being herself then Grecian. From this
> urge we find the hatred to those that would bring physical, mental
> or spiritual forces captive in any manner, or force issue with any
> individual, yet manifesting same much in any subject the entity
> wishes to discuss same. Gaining from this also the study of the
> physical forces in physical conditions.                4898-1

On another occasion, Cayce told a twenty–two–year–old journalist
that he had been firsthand witness to the Trojan War and had eventually settled in Crete, where he had served in the capacity of a counselor.
He had also been responsible for the construction of many statues that—
according to Edgar Cayce—still existed and had not yet been uncovered
at the time (1930):

> In the one before this we find in that period when that known as
> the Trojan wars. The entity among those of the isles that were
> defenders of the gate through which the armies of the leaders en-
> tered, or went *out* to do battle, and was of the gate keeper's house,
> and will contact many that were in that particular period. In the
> name Ioncolm. In the period the entity gained, for much of the
> entity's experience was given rather to that of contemplation than
> of activity. Hence the variations in the two experiences—so ex-
> tremes; and the mediator and the counselor was the entity during
> that period, and the entity lived many days in the land, and be-
> came—after the settling up in Crete—one of the *counselors* of
> the land. Many of those statutes, many of those as may yet be
> found in the isle, the entity had much to do with their construc-
> tion—especially as related to the telling of, or showing of, his-
> toric incidents during that period.                2896-1

According to the *Aeneid*, the Trojans arrived at Crete and began to build their new home, but sickness broke out among the people and the crops failed to present a harvest. One night Aeneas had a dream that he was to leave Crete and seek Hesperian (Italian) shores. Upon telling the dream to Anchises, the Trojan remembered that Cassandra had long ago prophesied that the Trojans would eventually settle there.

They set sail again. Their travels took them along the western coast of Greece where they encountered unusual creatures called the Harpies (half-woman and half-bird). Eventually, they passed by the coastline of Epirus and came to a small kingdom ruled by Andromache, the widow of Hector, and Helenus, Trojan soothsayer and Hector's surviving brother. The two had married and led a small group of Trojan refugees who had also survived the war. (Other legends suggest that Andromache had been forced to marry a Greek warrior-king after the death of her husband, or even Achilles' son Neoptolemus.) They sailed to Sicily where they encountered a marooned member of Ulysses' crew named Achaemenides who warned them of the danger of Polyphemus, the Cyclops. They continued their journey and while on the opposite coast, Aeneas' father Anchises died. It was there that King Acestes of Drepanum was hospitable to them because his mother was of Trojan descent. Finally, they left the Sicilian coast and sailed to Carthage, the home of Dido.

After discussing his wanderings, Aeneas and Dido went on a hunting trip where they were influenced by Venus and Juno to begin a scandalous and all-consuming love affair that caused both of them to forgot all their duties and obligations. Although Venus apparently helped the two to fall in love because of her love for her son, Juno's assistance was obviously to prevent the Trojans from reaching their goal of establishing a new kingdom.

For one year Aeneas stayed in Dido's palace enjoying pleasure and bounty but eventually Mercury (Hermes) was sent to remind Aeneas of the new kingdom he was to found. Aeneas tried to explain to Dido why he had to leave Carthage but she refused to listen. She was so overcome with sadness that she passed out and was carried back to her bedchamber by her maids. Aeneas was torn between following after her and giving her comfort or following through with his duty:

> Duty-bound, Aeneas, though he struggled with desire to calm and comfort her in all her pain, to speak to her and turn her mind from grief, and though he sighed his heart out, shaken still with love of her, yet took the course heaven gave him and went back to the fleet. (Fitzgerald, *Aeneid*, Book Four, lines 545-551)

Aeneas and his ships sailed while Dido slept. When she awoke and discovered what had happened and how her lover had simply left her, she killed herself atop a funeral pyre that also burned with Aeneas' effigy. She also predicted years of animosity between her people of Carthage and Aeneas' descendants. (As an aside, historically Carthage and Rome were bitter enemies until Rome finally destroyed the city in 146 B.C.)

Once again, the Trojans sailed to the Sicilian port of King Acestes where they took part in games of wrestling, racing, boxing, and archery as a means of commemorating the one-year anniversary of the death of Anchises. Meanwhile, Juno through the messenger goddess Iris made the Trojan women become upset for their years of wandering and caused them to set fire to the Trojan vessels.

Aeneas cried out to Jupiter for assistance, and the god caused rains to come down and squelch the fires. Although four ships were lost, the others appeared seaworthy. That night the ghost of Anchises appeared and told Aeneas to leave Sicily, travel to Cumae and consult the Sibyl, the priestess of Apollo, about what he was supposed to do. The priestess had gained her powers of prophecy from Apollo who had loved her and been spurned.

Because of her son's tribulations, Venus appealed to Neptune to assist the Trojans on the rest of their journey. Neptune pointed out that he had often been of assistance to Aeneas and asked only for the life of one Trojan to assure safe passage. As a result, the ship's navigator Palinurus fell asleep during the journey and slipped overboard, eventually drowning in the sea. After his death, Aeneas took control of the ship and guided the rest of the fleet to Italy.

As instructed, he went to the Sibyl's cave and declared his wish to visit Hades. During his visit with the Sibyl, she told him he had to fight one more war. She also took him to Hades, where he came in contact with Dido. Although Aeneas cried and asked his former lover for forgiveness, she snubbed him.

Aeneas moved on to a place for the blessed spirits called the Elysium, where he was met by his father Anchises who pointed out all of the countless souls who were waiting to be purified of their earthly sins. According to Anchises, after they were purged, many were to be reincarnated and born to bring glory to the future of Italy—Silvius (the unborn son of Aeneas, who would found Alba Longa); Romulus, Caesar, Brutus, Augustus Caesar, and so forth.

Afterward, Aeneas returned to his companions, led them to the mouth of the Tiber and then on to Latium, the home of the Latins, where their wanderings were to cease. Because of a prophecy that foretold the marriage of his only daughter to a foreign prince, King Latinus promised the hand of his daughter Lavinia for him to marry. Unfortunately, another Latin named Turnus already had feelings for Lavinia. Because he had long hoped to win her favors, he was extremely unhappy with the turn of events. Juno also became upset by the engagement and she tried to intervene and create a war but to no avail: "In spite of all the years which had elapsed since Paris scorned her attractions and bribes, Juno had not yet forgotten her hatred of the Trojan race . . . " (Guerber, pg. 373)

War finally threatened to break out between the Latins and the Trojans when Ascanius killed a pet stag that belonged to the daughter of the king's herdsman. When the onslaught of war appeared unavoidable, Aeneas sought and won an alliance with a man named Evander, who ruled the small town of Pallanteum, and his son Pallas. The friendship formed quickly because Pallanteum was already at war with the Latins.

Meanwhile, concerned for her son's safety, Venus caused Vulcan to create a suit of armor for him, just as the god had done previously for both Achilles and Ulysses.

Battles between the two sides ensued when the Latins first attacked the Trojan camp and then the Trojans turned to attack the Latin camp. It was only through the intervention of Jupiter that the Trojan ships were preserved from Turnus' attack. The two forces battled without a decisive victor but slaughter occurred on both sides. According to legend, the mighty, female, virgin warrior named Camilla came to help the Latins but was killed by the Trojans. At one point, Turnus mercilessly killed the young Pallas. After a truce enabling both sides to bury their dead, Turnus and Aeneas finally met in hand-to-hand combat:

> At length the final conflict took place between Aeneas and Turnus. Turnus had avoided the contest as long as he could, but at last, impelled by the ill success of his arms and by the murmurs of his followers, he braced himself to the conflict. It could not be doubtful. On the side of Aeneas were the expressed decree of destiny, the aid of his goddess-mother at every emergency, and impenetrable armour fabricated by Vulcan, at her request, for her son. Turnus, on the other hand, was deserted by his celestial allies, Juno having been expressly forbidden by Jupiter to assist him any longer. Turnus threw his lance, but it recoiled harmless from the shield of Aeneas. The Trojan hero then threw his, which penetrated the shield of Turnus, and pierced his thigh. Then Turnus' fortitude forsook him and he begged for mercy; and Aeneas would have given him life, but at the instant his eye fell on the belt of Pallas, which Turnus had taken from the slaughtered youth. Instantly his rage revived and exclaiming, "Pallas immolates thee with this blow," he thrust him through with the sword. (Bulfinch, pg. 263)

After the war, Aeneas married Lavinia, and the Trojans and the Latins became peaceful neighbors; in time, the two would become one people. In this place the descendants of Troy would give birth to a new empire.

According to Roman mythology, Aeneas founded the city of Lavinium, naming it after his wife. Their son Silvius founded the city of Alba Longa, into which the twins Romulus and Remus were born to the Vestal Virgin Ilia after her marriage to Mars several hundred years later. Because of a cruel stepfather, the twins were discarded, nursed by a she-wolf, and eventually raised by a shepherd and his wife. In time they would found a new city. It was a disagreement over the city's borders that caused Romulus to kill his brother. That new city was Rome, of which legend suggests Romulus became the first leader in 753 B.C.

So ends the journey of the Trojans who, according to legend, became the Romans.

# 5

# HEINRICH SCHLIEMANN AND ARCHAEOLOGICAL RESEARCH AT TROY

lthough Heinrich Schliemann (1822–1890) is generally credited with being the discoverer of Troy, his life and work have become the subjects of frequent criticism, denunciation, and numerous attempts to separate fact from fiction. In addition to his archaeological excavations, history has also found that he was not above breaking the law as a means of achieving his goals, nor was he above lying, blatant self-promotion, and even theft. A self-made millionaire, Schliemann underwrote his own archaeological work; unfortunately, he also created inconsistencies in his biographical and archaeological information and destroyed important archaeological ruins in pursuit of his personal interests.

Because of Schliemann's propensity to exaggerate the truth as well as outright lie, critics state that "it is not always possible to distinguish myth from reality" when examining his life's work and personal records. Keeping this in mind, throughout much of his life Schliemann was a voluminous writer; his own notes, books, records and letters contain a vast array of written records and materials:

> **There are eleven books, the so-called autobiography, eighteen travel diaries, 20,000 papers, 60,000 letters, business records, postcards, telegrams . . . there are also 175 volumes of excavation notebooks, though forty-six more are missing, including important ones from Troy, Orchomenos and Tiryns . . . (Wood, page 48 )**

In spite of his many shortcomings, however, even his critics generally agree that he was brilliant in a number of respects. Largely self-educated, he showed an amazing propensity for languages, in addition to his native German, he eventually mastered English, Russian, French, Dutch, Portuguese, Spanish, and Italian, as well as ancient and modern Greek. He also possessed an innate talent for business, enabling him to amass a large fortune and retire at the age of forty-one. It was only after his retirement that he devoted himself to the study of archaeology.

Heinrich Schliemann was born on January 6, 1822, in Neu–Bukow in Germany. His father was a pastor who had reportedly committed adultery and allegedly squandered church funds through embezzlement—activities that disgraced both the pastor and his family. His mother died when he was nine and his father was suspended from the Protestant church one year later. After his father lost his job, he and his siblings were sent to live with an uncle. According to Schliemann, even before losing his job, his father often complained of the family's financial woes and poverty. Perhaps the family's troubling economic situation became part of the impetus that, for decades, drove Schliemann in search of financial independence.

According to Schliemann, his lifelong interest in Troy came as a result of a Christmas present he received from his father at the age of seven, eight, or ten, depending upon which version of the tale you read. The present was Ludwig Jerrer's *Illustrated History of the World*. The book contained a picture of Troy in flames and showed the surviving warrior

Aeneas fleeing from the doomed city carrying his father on his back and holding his son by the hand. The picture showed Troy as a city with enormous stone walls, allegedly causing young Heinrich to point out to his father: "The walls are much too large to be destroyed by fire, there must be something left." Schliemann claimed it was at that very moment he decided to discover for himself one day the city and walls of Troy. However, in spite of Schliemann's voluminous writings covering many decades, no written record of this story exists until 1868, his forty-sixth year. What is perhaps suspicious about the date is that it corresponds to the same year Schliemann met Frank Calvert, an individual who scholars now point to as the source of Schliemann's information and inspiration to dig at Hisarlik—the site of Troy's discovery.

According to Schliemann's autobiographical information, when he was seven he met and fell in love with Minna Meincke, the daughter of a local farmer. For two years they were inseparable and swore, as children, to marry and spend the rest of their lives together. Unfortunately, they were separated when Schliemann went to live with his uncle.

Shortly after his father lost his job, Schliemann's classical education came to a close because his father was unable to pay for private schooling. He briefly attended public school but was forced to drop out at fourteen because of his father's continued financial difficulties. At that point Heinrich Schliemann became apprenticed to a grocer.

By all accounts, he hated both the man he had to work for as well as the work he had to perform in the shop. While children his own age were outside playing, he was forced to sweep floors, dust and arrange counters, carry heavy casks, and sell herring, dry goods, butter, milk, oil, candles, and potato whiskey. His dream was to become wealthy and marry Minna, but his wages were small and his opportunities for advancement and study seemingly nonexistent. However, Schliemann later reported that it was while working at the shop that he became further inspired to search for Homer's Troy. Known for his tendency to tell exaggerated stories, Schliemann in his autobiography describes how he heard Homeric Greek for the first time while apprenticed to the grocer:

. . . as long as I live, I shall never forget the evening when a

> drunken miller came into the shop. His name was Herman
> Nieferhöffer. He was the son of a Protestant clergyman . . . Dissat-
> isfied with his lot, the young man gave himself up to drink, which,
> however, had not made him forget his Homer; for on the evening
> that he entered the shop he recited to us about a hundred lines of
> the poet, observing the rhythmic cadence of the verses. Although I
> did not understand a syllable, the melodious sound of the words
> made a deep impression upon me, and I wept bitter tears over my
> unhappy fate. Three times over did I get him to repeat to me those
> divine verses, rewarding his trouble with three glasses of whiskey,
> which I bought with the few pence that made up my whole fortune.
> From that moment I never ceased to pray God that by His grace I
> might yet have the happiness of learning Greek. (Schliemann,
> pg. 7)

Eventually, he was able to leave the grocers and travel to Hamburg
and finally Amsterdam. His first big break came in 1842 when he was
employed by a counting house. His job was to stamp bills of exchange
and get them cashed in town. Frugal with his money, he spent funds
only for bare necessities: his living expenses and his education.

In 1844, he obtained a job with Herr Schroder's import and export
business. Because of his negotiating skills and his aptitude for languages,
he was stationed in Russia in 1846 and began amassing a personal fortune through his commissions as the chief representative of the trading
firm. When he had finally established himself in St. Petersburg, he wrote
to Germany to ask for the hand of Minna in marriage; he was devas-
tated to find that she had already married a local farmer. Afterward, he
devoted himself even further to the pursuit of money.

One of his younger brothers had gone to America and amassed a
small fortune in banking in California. Unfortunately, the young man
died unexpectedly from Typhus in 1850. For that reason Schliemann left
for California the same year and settled in Sacramento. He set himself
up as a buyer of gold dust and became even wealthier, but he was
lonely. His first stay in America was brief.

He returned to St. Petersburg and married a Russian girl by the name of Ekaterina Lishin. Almost immediately, he knew he had made a mistake and he considered returning to the United States. After his unhappy marriage, he spent most of his time focusing on business. During his free time he learned to read and write modern and ancient Greek. Eventually his business concerns took him to China and Japan. Throughout his business life, he made money in indigo, sulfur, and lead. He had made money in California gold and a small fortune during the Crimean War. During one period or another, he had large investments in Russia, Cuba, Germany, and the United States. By 1855, his personal worth was around one million dollars—a huge sum at the time. In spite of his personal successes, however, he was dissatisfied with his life and sought some other outlet for his talents and his life's direction:

> In the late 1850s he seems to have wanted to break away from his business career into more intellectual pursuits in order to gain respectability. His first hopes were to become a landed proprietor, devoting himself to agriculture. When this failed, he wanted to turn to some sort of activity in a scientific field, perhaps philology [the study of languages], but was soon discouraged . . . Like many European people in the nineteenth century he knew Homer and loved his tale, but it was probably only his visit to Greece and Troy in the summer of 1868—and his meeting with Frank Calvert— which gave Schliemann the inspiration to turn to archaeology, and the idea of discovering Homer's Troy by excavation. (Wood, page 49)

Although unhappy with his wife, he had three children with her. Because of his wealth and his restlessness, he began thinking about retiring but knew he would not be happy simply being idle. During his worldwide travels he came to Paris in 1866 and for a time considered remaining:

> At the age of forty-four, he had decided what he wanted to be: he would become a philologist, a student of languages, going to classes at the Sorbonne, and in the intervals between attending

lectures he would publish his book on China and Japan.

He had made three fortunes, visited half the countries in the world, sired three children by a frigid wife, learned twelve or thirteen languages, collected a vast library, but even now, grown gray and weary, he had no idea what he would do with his life. (Payne, page 90)

He loved Paris but in spite of his pleading, his wife refused to move there with the children; she remained in St. Petersburg. While at the Sorbonne, he attended some lectures on archaeology. Years later, after having met Frank Calvert and having embarked on his own archaeological investigations, he remained physically separated from his family. At one point Schliemann's son Sergey would write a letter to his father and confess that he was not doing well in school. Not known for his empathy, Schliemann used himself as an example to try to convince the boy to do better:

It was very sad to hear you have not been progressing. In this life one must progress continually, otherwise one becomes discouraged. Try then to follow the example of your father who, in all the positions he has occupied, has always proved how much a man can accomplish provided he has fierce energy. I performed miracles during the four years 1842-1846 in Amsterdam. I did what no one else has ever done and no one else could ever do. Then I became a merchant in St. Petersburg, and no merchant was ever so accomplished or so prudent. Then I became a traveler, but not an ordinary traveler—I was a traveler *par excellence*. No other merchant in St. Petersburg has ever written a scientific work, but I wrote one which was translated into four languages, a book which became the object of universal admiration. Today I am an archaeologist, and all Europe and America are dazzled by my discovery of the ancient city of Troy—that Troy which the archaeologists of all countries have searched in vain for two thousand years ... (Payne, pages 136-137)

Attempting to soothe his feelings of restlessness, he made his way to

Greece in the summer of 1868 and pursued archaeology. His first excavations were at Mount Aetios, where he found the foundation of a
building, cremation urns, a clay goddess and a knife. He also dug at
Pinarbaşi—the site scholars often associated with Troy. But he went away
disappointed and disillusioned. He was encouraged to seek out the advice of Frank Calvert, a man who was reputed to know more about the
area and the possible existence of Troy than any other individual.

After his meeting with Calvert, Schliemann vowed to launch an archaeological investigation for Troy at Hisarlik. He returned to Paris and
while there, in December 1868, he wrote Calvert a letter essentially asking for advice and also demonstrating his lack of knowledge in the field
of archaeology. The letter included nineteen questions to which
Schliemann requested a swift reply:

1　When is the best time to begin work?
2　Is it not advisable to begin as early as possible in Spring?
3　I am very susceptible to fever; is there much apprehension of
　　same in Spring?
4　What medicines have I to take with me?
5　Must I take a servant with me? or can I get a very trustworthy
　　one in Athens? Probably it is better to have a faithful Greek
　　who speaks Turkish.
6　Have I to take a tent and iron bedstead and pillow with me
　　from Marseille? for all the houses in the plain of Troy are in-
　　fested with vermin.
7　Please give me an exact statement of all the *implements* of
　　whatever kind and of *all the necessaries* which you advise me
　　to take with me.
8　Do I require pistols, dagger and rifle?
9　Is there no obstacle on the part of the landowners to excavate
　　the artificial hill?
10　Can I get laborers enough, where and at what wages?
11　How many can I employ? It is better to take Greeks or Turks?
12　In how much time do you think I can dig away the artificial
　　mountain?

13  At what cost?

14  You suggested to dig first a tunnel! But I am sure this is not practical, for if the hill really consists of ruins of ancient temples and walls, the cyclopean stones will impede the tunnel being made.

15  What has led you to conclude that the hill is artificial?

16  You indicate the dimensions as 700 feet square; a Frenchman would understand you 26½ feet long and as much in breadth; but I think you meet 700 feet long and the same in breadth, which in the French mode of calculating, would make 490,000 square feet. But in my book I have stated the length and breadth with 233 meters, which would make about 54,000 square meters.

17  What is the high [height?] of the artificial mount to be taken away?

18  I think the best plan is to take a credit on Constantinople banker, who adds it to a firm in the Dardanelles so that I am not bothered and can take out at the Dardanelles what I require.

19  What sort of a hat is best against scorching sun?

(Payne, pages 113-115)

Although evidence clearly suggests that Heinrich Schliemann owed his inspiration to dig at Hisarlik to Frank Calvert, Schliemann would later deny that Calvert had anything to do with the idea.

Frank Calvert (1828–1908) was an unassuming scholar who made perhaps one of the greatest unknown contributions to archaeology in history. Calvert and his family had long been interested in antiquities and the story of the Trojan War. Although English, the family had a farm at New Ilium, about five miles from Hisarlik. As a result, Calvert knew the area better than most individuals and was eager to share his theories on the location of Troy with anyone, including Heinrich Schliemann.

Long interested in archaeology and history, Calvert by 1853 had done archaeological fieldwork in which he had located the city of Ophryneion (according to some legends the location of Hector's tomb), including its harbor and acropolis. He also made important discoveries at Colonae and various sites throughout the Troad—the northwestern region of Asia Minor. Over time, he and his brother Frederick had also amassed an impressive collection of vases from numerous sites that came to the attention of various scholars and archaeologists (Allen, pg. 69–70). Frank Calvert had a longstanding and personal interest in discovering Troy. For that reason, years before ever meeting Schliemann he had pursued archaeological excavations at numerous locations including Pinarbaşi.

Throughout the nineteenth century it was generally agreed that if Troy had ever actually existed, it was probably somewhere in the Troad region of Turkey. Tradition had also long stated that the Trojan War occurred in the area of Hisarlik, a name that means, place of the fort. The site is located in northwestern Turkey about four miles from the Aegean Sea and the Dardanelles. Legend also suggested that the tomb of Achilles could be found on a prominent mound known as Beşik Tepe, which stands approximately five miles from where Troy was eventually located. Here, it was claimed, great warriors such as Alexander, Xerxes, and others came to pay their respects. As if to the confirm the legendary accounts, archaeological investigations at Beşik Tepe eventually uncovered Greek graves, cremations, and pottery, all believed to be from the thirteenth century B.C., a date corresponding to the Trojan War (Wood, pg. 168).

Although Calvert had identified various areas in the region over the years as being possible sites for Homeric Troy, as early as 1864 he had turned his attention to Hisarlik (Wood, pg. 43)—six years before Schliemann's discovery. That same year, Calvert purchased the northern portion of Hisarlik and the following year conducted his own trial excavations in four places. In fact, Calvert owned approximately one-half of the land upon which Schliemann eventually "found" Troy.

Although the site at Hisarlik had long been rumored to be one of the possible locations of Troy, no one had begun excavations in the area until Frank Calvert. Previously, Charles Maclaren (1782–1866), a brilliant journalist, editor, and amateur geologist, who had never visited the area, became convinced as early as 1822 that Troy was at Hisarlik. Unfortunately, by the time of Troy's actual discovery in 1870, Maclaren was already dead.

Calvert believed that the Hisarlik was an artificial mound, layered with ruins of centuries of temples and palaces. Eventually, his work on the site located a Greek temple dedicated to Athena and a wall of the city of Lysimachus, which had been built by one of Alexander the Great's generals. It was a classical city wall that was destroyed by Schliemann's excavations a few years later. Excavations would reveal ultimately that Calvert had come within yards of the northeastern portion of what would one day be identified as Troy VI.

Calvert's fascination with the possibility of finding Troy led him repeatedly to seek the financial backing necessary for such an investigation from a variety of sources, including the British Museum. Unfortunately, he could never acquire the funds necessary to launch an all-out archaeological investigation. A financial scandal involving his brother Frederick and Frederick's forced bankruptcy had essentially blacklisted the Calvert name. As a result, Frank was unable to procure the finances he needed to launch an archaeological dig for Troy at Hisarlik. In spite of his failure, Calvert remained convinced that the site would eventually reveal the Troy that had long been a part of legend:

> Frank Calvert strongly believed in the history of Homers account of Troy. Years previously he publicly had dismissed Pinarbaşi as its site, along with other theories of its location. He had become convinced, instead, that Troy lay at Hisarlik. He believed that over the preceding years, while excavating small sections of the land that he owned there, he had made finds that would prove it, although at present he was unable to afford the effort to do so. Calvert, the experienced excavator who understood the stratigraphy and the buildup of cultural debris, convinced the defeated Schliemann, who had resources more adequate for the task of excavation. Calvert always had been generous with his knowledge . . . he seized on Schliemann's financial strength to carry out the excavations he had hoped to conduct himself. (Allen, pg. 8)

Beginning with Heinrich Schliemann's archaeological investigations in 1870, the first of a series of Trojan settlements was uncovered. Eventually, these investigations would reveal nine phases of activity, built one upon the other, later numbered Troy I through Troy IX. These various levels also included forty-nine subdivisions and provided evidence that human civilization had dwelt upon the site from at least 3600 B.C. to around 1500 A.D. Interestingly enough, as if to confirm Homer's statement that the people of Troy were known for their work with horses, archaeological investigations at Troy VI were found to contain a great number of horse bones (Wood, pg. 166).

In his autobiographical accounts, Schliemann claimed that it was Homer's *Iliad* that guided him to the site of Troy and not Frank Calvert. In fact, for the rest of their twenty-year relationship, Schliemann took great lengths to minimize Calvert's role in the discovery. For example, Calvert had granted Schliemann permission to dig on the eastern half of the mound at Hisarlik—property owned by Calvert himself. However, Schliemann launched his dig on the western half of the mound without permission from the Turkish owners and without a government permit. In a letter announcing the first week of excavations at Hisarlik, Schliemann rationalized his actions by stating: "Knowing in advance that the Turkish owners would refuse to give me permission I did not ask them." (Allen, pg. 128)

In April of 1870, Heinrich Schliemann's archaeological dig for Troy began. Amazingly, by the end of the first day of work, his laborers had uncovered the foundation of a building sixty feet long by forty feet wide. Within a few days of the find, the Turks who actually owned the property arrived and inquired what Schliemann was up to, claiming that he had no right to be there. Schliemann argued back but to no avail. However, the Turks were interested in the heavy blocks of stone he had unearthed, which they intended to use for a bridge they were building over the Simois River. After discussing the matter, they let Schliemann continue his excavation in exchange for the stones.

When Schliemann finally persuaded Turkish government authorities to grant him a permit to dig at Hisarlik, he had to agree to three conditions: (1) He would have to pay for the entire excavation; (2) no existing structures could be demolished—any finds upon the site had to be left intact; and, (3) he had to split half of his finds with the Turkish archaeological museum. History has found that Schliemann only abided by the first condition.

In his personal life, Schliemann eventually obtained an American divorce from his Russian wife. Around the same time he had asked a friend of his in Greece to pick out a bride for him. He wanted someone beautiful, poor, well educated, an enthusiast of Homer's, and in possession of dark hair and a loving heart. His friend, Vimpos, collected photographs of available girls and sent them to Indianapolis, where Schliemann had gone to acquire American citizenship and his divorce from Ekatrina. It was the photo of Greek–born Sophia Engastromenos that stared out at him from among the others. In 1869, when his divorce was final, he married Sophia.

At the time of their marriage, she was seventeen; he was in his late forties and more than thirty years her senior. When he asked her why she was willing to marry him, her reply was that it was because he was a very rich man. Although hurt by her words, Schliemann married her within a month after their meeting.

Returning to Schliemann's archaeological work, in time his mound of Hisarlik would become riddled with trenches and long corridors in the search for treasure. Between 1871 and 1873, he undertook three major campaigns at the site, employing anywhere between eighty and two hundred laborers. Schliemann haphazardly removed hundreds of tons of earth and debris, destroying walls of cities that he thought irrelevant to his find. Some of his most vocal critics contend that Schliemann didn't discover Troy, he pillaged it. His critics also claim that his main aim was publicity and achieving prominence.

Schliemann dug through several layers of cities at Hisarlik and announced that the second city from the bottom was none other than Homer's fabled city of Troy. However, later it was discovered that Homeric Troy was at a higher level. He found gold jewelry at the level of Troy II and took pictures of his wife, Sophia, wearing the pieces, which he erroneously called "King Priam's Treasure." In fact, many of his finds were dubbed with names that would heighten their sensational appeal, such as: "the ashes of Odysseus," "the sepulchre of Agamemnon," and "the Palace of Priam."

Although he had agreed to split any finds with the Turkish museum, Schliemann secretly smuggled hoards of treasure out of Troy. It was only in the face of a lawsuit filed by the Turkish government in 1875 that Schliemann was forced to pay 50,000 francs as compensation for the government's share (Allen, pg. 177). Afterwards, much of the treasure seemingly disappeared. However, years later, in 1996, after the end of the Cold War, the treasures of gold, silver, jewelry, and weapons taken by Schliemann from Hisarlik were put on public display. They had been hidden for more than fifty years in the basement of Moscow's Pushkin State Museum of Fine Arts.

Schliemann returned to the area again in 1878 and 1879, after uncovering major finds of ancient Greek civilization at Mycenae. His work at Mycenae included excavating the tombs of Mycenaean kings in Greece, unearthing the remains of a great palace in Tiryns, and conducting excavations at Ithaca. Actually, before Schliemann, the civilization of preclassical Greece (ca. 6000 to 1000 B.C.) was not even known to have existed. He made what would be his last dig between 1889 and 1890, the year of his death. Schliemann had returned repeatedly to the site in an effort to find indisputable evidence that the Troy of Hisarlik was the Troy of Homer.

Heinrich Schliemann died from complications and general debilitation after an unsuccessful operation for a painfully inflamed chronic ear infection. He was buried in his mausoleum in Athens, characteristically inscribed with the motto: "For the hero Schliemann." Conversely, Frank Calvert died in 1908, in his eightieth year, without ever being recognized for his contribution to the excavation of Troy. In fact, until the discovery of various documents and a reexamination of the facts in the last quarter of the twentieth century, his involvement was generally regarded as "a family myth" (Allen, pg. 246). From all accounts, it appears that history will eventually rewrite the notion that Schliemann was the sole discoverer of Troy.

In spite of the fact that Schliemann never discovered concrete evidence to prove Hisarlik was the location of Homeric Troy, his work did demonstrate that the central places discussed in Homer's story were, in fact, centermost during that period in ancient Greece. He may have also been among the first individuals to correlate some of the area's topography and native livestock with Homer's descriptions in the *Iliad*. In an appendix to his classic work, *Ilios*, documenting his discoveries at Troy, Schliemann had a noted anthropologist, Professor Rudolf Virchow (1821–1902), from the University of Berlin, discuss some of the similarities:

> **I do not refer merely to Homer's oft-noticed characteristic descriptions . . . but far more to his almost surprising knowledge of the meteorology of the district, of the flora and fauna, and the social peculiarities of its population. Three thousand years have not sufficed to produce any noteworthy alteration in these things. The clouds are still drawn in the same courses as are described in the *Iliad*, and the storms gather on the same mountain-tops as in Homer's time. The number of wild beasts have grown gradually less, and the camel and the turkey have been added to the tame stock, but the native species are unchanged. The flowers, shrubs, and trees, mentioned in the poem, still grow on the river-banks and the mountain uplands . . . (Schliemann, pg. 675)**

Years later, in February 2003, a public relations release from the University of Delaware would carry the headline: "UD researcher uncovers classical truth about ancient Troy," and cite the work of Professor of Geology John C. Kraft in noting similarities between Homer's story and the geography of the area:

> **Combining an interest in the classics with expertise in the sedimentary geology that defines coastlines, a University of Delaware researcher has discovered that Homer's "Iliad" presents an accurate account of the geography of ancient Troy, information that may end a centuries long debate.[6]**

---

[6]University of Delaware, Office of Public Relations Release, February 27, 2003

After Schliemann's passing, his early successors at Troy included excavations by William Dörpfeld (1890–1894) and Carl Blegen (1932–1938). Dörpfeld was an archaeologist who had assisted Schliemann for more than ten years. A few years after Schliemann's death, Dörpfeld returned to Troy and dug at the southern end of Hisarlik. The Kaiser and Sophia Schliemann, Heinrich's widow, financed his work. The dig lasted two years and eventually uncovered a find more glorious than anything Schliemann had discovered during his repeated attempts:

> . . . he uncovered 300 yards of the city wall, sometimes buried under as much as 50 feet of earth and debris and overlain by the ruins of later cities. In the north-east corner there was an immense angular watchtower, still standing 25 feet above the rock . . . The city itself was beautifully made in sections . . . There was a gate on the east, protected by a long overlapping wall, near to which was the base of a large square tower built of beautifully fitted limestone blocks . . . On the south was an important gate with another massive tower fronted by stone bases . . .
>
> Surely, this was the city reflected in the epic—a "well built" city with wide streets, beautiful walls and great gates just as the *Iliad* had told. (Wood, pgs. 89-91)

Carl Blegen (1877–1971) worked at Hisarlik from 1932 to 1938. Through Blegen's work it was discovered that a great earthquake had destroyed the enormous walls of Troy VI. Further investigations revealed that the successor to Troy VI, known as Troy VII, had experienced an all-out siege, probably within a generation of the quake. The site showed evidence of cramped living conditions, isolation from the outside world, and even a public bakery, which Blegen referred to as both a "soup kitchen" and a "snack bar." The public bakery, Blegen theorized, had been used to dispense food to the Trojan warriors in between back-and-forth journeys to the front lines. It became clear that concrete evidence of Homer's Trojan War had finally been found:

**Everywhere their city was marked by the ravages of fire, buried in**

**masses of burned mudbrick, charred wood and debris . . . There was little doubt that it had come from the hand of man. In the doorway of a house were found parts of a human skeleton covered in burnt timbers, stones and debris from the houses which had collapsed on the victims; in places the heaped ashes and wreckage were 5 feet deep. In the street outside the snack bar was part of a skull; remnants of another skull was found further to the west. In the burned rubbish covering a house outside the eastern citadel wall was the jawbone of a human skull crushed by stone . . . [Overall Blegen's discovery seemed to prove that Troy VIIa had been] a threatened community desperately laying in supplies to withstand a siege, and then the evidence of their final destruction. (Wood, pgs. 115-116)**

Blegen would eventually report:

**We believe that Troy VIIa has yielded actual evidence showing that the town was subjected to siege, capture and destruction by hostile forces at some time in the general period assigned by Greek tradition to the Trojan War, and that it may safely be identified as the Troy of Priam and of Homer. (Wood, pg. 114)**

In more recent archaeological work, beginning in 1988 and throughout the 1990s, Professor Manfred Korfmann of Germany's Tübingen University served as head of excavations for the area. Korfmann also investigated Schliemann's archaeological treasures at the Pushkin Museum. Rather than trying to prove the existence of Homeric Troy, one of Korfmann's goals was to simply understand what occurred on this strategic Bronze Age site. His excavations, and the work of others, have shown that there have been many "Trojan wars" in the area. Korfmann eventually found evidence of a fire and a "military event" in the ashes of Troy VII. Eventually, carbon 14 dating placed the catastrophe as occurring around 1180 B.C. (Allen, pg. 259)—a date that corresponds amazingly with the legendary timing for the fall of Troy, which has long been dated as having occurred in 1184 B.C.

# 6

# ADDITIONAL PSYCHIC INSIGHTS
## OF THE TROJAN PERIOD

s has already been discussed, the Edgar Cayce material parallels some of the information from the Trojan Myth that is contained in history, legend, and the works of individuals like Homer and Virgil. During the twenty–year period between 1923 and 1943, Cayce gave sixty readings to forty-five individuals that explored the period of the Trojan War. The purpose of that exploration was primarily to provide those individuals, including Cayce himself, with insights into abilities, talents, shortcomings, and relationships that were inextricably connected to previous incarnations.

In addition to confirming insights from the Trojan Myth that have long been recited, much like an eyewitness observer, Cayce was also able to detail information and people not recorded by history. From Cayce's clairvoyant perception of the past, individuals like Achilles, Hector, Helen, and others were flesh–and–blood personalities who faced extraordinary events that, in time, would become the basis of legend.

In an effort to explore some of the Edgar Cayce material regarding the Trojan Myth in greater detail, four characters stand out as having been central to Cayce's version of the events. In addition to Achilles, Hector, and Helen, the character of Xenon plays an important role, per–haps not so much in shaping the course of the war but certainly in impacting the life story of Edgar Cayce himself. Cayce believed that he had been Xenon during the same period when Achilles, Helen, Hector, and the others walked the earth.

## Xenon: readings 294–8, 294–9, 294–19, 294–161, 294–183

The Edgar Cayce readings first suggested in November 1923 that Cayce himself had been alive during the Greek–Trojan conflict; how–ever, it would not be until three months later, the following February, that he was able to explore that information in greater detail during his first life reading—a reading that discussed his soul's journey through a series of incarnations.

The reading stated that Cayce had been a soldier and one of the defenders of the gate during the Trojan War. Prior to the war, he had been a student, a chemist, a sculptor, and an artisan. The information also stated that his name during that period had been Xenon, and that there were many individuals with whom he had been familiar at that time that would reappear in the present (294–8). In May 1924, Cayce mentioned the same Trojan incarnation in passing, during a reading detailing a previous incarnation he had experienced in France (294–9). It wasn't until February 1925 that a follow–up life reading briefly men–tioned the Trojan incarnation again by stating that some of the "urges" he had acquired during his life as Xenon, including his tendency to have a quick temper, needed to be "overcome in the present." (294–19)

On September 19, 1933, Cayce awoke from a lengthy dream in which he remembered seeing himself as Xenon and witnessing the final battle between Achilles and Hector—individuals that he recognized as Morton

Blumenthal [900] and Arthur Lammers [5717] in the present (294–161). As will be discussed, both men had a major impact on the Cayce work. By this time, various readings had painted an entirely different picture of the Greek and Trojan heroes, suggesting that contrary to legend it was Achilles who was beloved by Greeks and Trojans alike and that Hector had been viewed as a cruel and vengeful dictator who had apparently stolen the throne from its rightful heir.

For example, in May 1929, during a reading given to a thirty–two–year–old commercial banker, Cayce told the individual that during the Trojan period there had been "wars within and without." In addition to the invading Greek army, the city had become divided over Hector's reign. At that time, although one of Troy's defenders, the banker had been among those who had banded together under Achilles in an effort to overthrow the city's despised leader:

> In the one before this we find in that period when there were wars within and without, known as the Trojan period. The entity then among those who defended the city, and was among those that rose with him that destroyed the usurper, or the one without heart—Hector; and the entity gained through this experience, and lost in other portions of self's own aggrandizement of power gained. Gaining when in service and in acting the *ideal* that impelled many during that period. Losing in meting to others that that was disliked in self. Hence that of the dislike of littleness in self or others, and of the hanger-on.                              2886-1

Perhaps because of the demands on his time and various crises that impacted his life, it was not until July 1935 that Edgar Cayce finally obtained a reading for himself that focused entirely on his Xenon incarnation. During the course of that reading, Cayce stated that because of Xenon's actions at the time, at least from the perspective of soul growth and development, his life had been, in part, "a failure in its activity."

Altering slightly from the date legend generally associates with the Trojan War, Cayce gave the period of Xenon's life as being from "eleven fifty–eight to ten twelve [eleven twelve? 1112?] B.C.," suggesting that he

had died at forty–six years of age. Although elsewhere the readings
state that Helen was literally kidnapped and taken from Greece to Troy,
Cayce's own reading goes on to suggest that these two powers had been
looking for an excuse to go to war. In other words, the kidnapping of
Helen was simply a pretext for a war that had long been desired on
both sides:

> So in that experience strife was bred among the Grecians and Tro-
> jans, who were at the period those units of power that sought a
> justification; or an excuse that there might be a meeting of the
> strength as to that condition or experience that is ever combative.
> No matter what terms may be used for the expression, there is
> ever the combativeness between Right and Wrong, or Power and
> Strength, or the irresistible and immovable; they are ever and con-
> stantly vying one with another.                              294-183

Although part of the rationale for war had been an effort to bring
freedom to the common people, other readings suggest that rather than
freedom, the war had instead promoted revenge and conflict among
many average citizens. The reading given to a thirty–nine–year–old secretary in 1934 discussed this result, as well as the individual's own experiences during the Trojan lifetime:

> Before that we find the entity was in that land through which much
> has been presented by the poets of old, in both the beauty and yet
> the savagery of those people in the Trojan activity, when Achilles
> and Hector in their activities brought to many of the common
> people only the revenge one upon another through the relations
> caused one with another.
>
> The entity then was associated rather with the Achilles influ-
> ences that finally overcame the Hector forces through the death of
> Hector. Achilles then was among those that made for the associa-
> tions with the entity that brought the entity's activities into the
> experience of many of the leaders of the period. And art, as well
> as literature through the entity's activity, brought much to those

peoples—as there was the restoring of peace among those of the isles and those of that land.

Then the entity was in the name Schulen, or Hulen—for it was both ways, as would be interpreted in the present.

In that experience the entity gained and lost; yet from that sojourn much of the determination arises, innately, that is oft expressed in the entity's activity. Yet the beauty, the tenderness of heart, the relationships that may come about through the power of might and strength through *right*, bring to the entity an activity that answers for the purposefulness in self.                    692-1

During the same period, however, from Cayce's perspective there were individuals that gained great strides at a soul level, even in the face of adversity. For example, a twenty-six-year-old man was told that he had originally been a Trojan and a defender of the gate and had been seriously injured. After the city was overtaken by the Greeks, however, he learned "brotherly love" in response to the care and healing that was given to him by the very people who had once been his enemies:

In the one before this we find in the days when there was war in the Eastern country, known then as Trojan War. The entity then the soldier in that land, and a defender at the gates against the lead of the peoples who were brought in possession through the action of Achilles. The entity then in the name Thesiolups, and the entity *gained* in that period, through the things suffered at the time of the injury to the body, for with care and attention given during this period the entity gained much of brotherly love, as was manifested, and as has been and will ever remain a condition in earth to be sought, studied and understood, and is as the key, or the sine qua non of the successes of secret organizations, which the entity likes and desires to be a portion of many. In the period the entity came in contact with many of high estate, *mentally*, and the desires of the entity in the recuperative period brought much learning to the entity. In the present urge there is seen the desire

**to spread learning; not as that of excess, but the good it (learning) will bring to others.                                          4180-1**

According to Cayce's own information, because his soul had previously excelled during experiences in ancient Egypt and ancient Persia in which conflicting forces had been brought together in peaceful cooperation, he had purposefully chosen to incarnate in Troy in an effort to be a helpful influence in the long–brewing Grecian–Trojan conflict. In fact, one reading discussing the development of human consciousness suggested that over time Cayce had learned and "tempered to give self" from a truly universal perspective (5755–1), enabling him to see the broader picture. Unfortunately, rather than becoming a mediator in the struggle, the reading states that he had instead been "forced" against his will, presumably through the action of King Hector, to become an active participant in the conflict. In other words, Xenon had been essentially drafted into service as a soldier and a defender at the gate instead of the mediator and calming influence he had been born to be.

Because of past–life experiences in which the soul of Edgar Cayce had developed a heightened sense of intuition, for a time Xenon may have been able to use his psychic ability to help defend the city. In any event, the reading suggests that he and many of the guards had developed incredible physical prowess, and that in spite of repeated attempts, the Greek army had been unable to break through the city gates. The information goes on to say that the Greeks (and the conspiring Trojans) eventually used something that had, up to that time, not really been a part of Cayce's soul experience—encountering lies and deceit in others. That conspiracy included the Trojan horse and, as a result, Xenon became one of those personally responsible for allowing the horse into the city (apparently even his intuition failed to see through the deception):

**In *this* manner, then, did the entity fail. And with the failure came the experience of being an outcast, as one dishonored, as one thought little of; at last losing self through self-destruction in those periods when there arose again the conditions or activities of those**

> in power, when Achilles rose to the strength to meet the needs in
> those particular experiences.
>
> And hence there was brought the falling away. This is how; this
> is the manner.                                                    294-183

Regardless of the fact that many of the Trojans apparently despised
their leader and had participated in the rebellion, because of feeling
shamed for his failure to fulfill his duty, Cayce, as Xenon, took his own
life. It was an act of "self–effacement" that would remain with him at a
soul level, becoming one of the greatest stumbling blocks he had to
overcome in the present. In the language of the readings: "And this is
the *great* barrier, the great experience which the entity must meet in the
present, the one thing *most* needed in the experience first; that is, a
regeneration from that experience." Meeting that experience in the
present apparently included dealing with a series of personal and pro-
fessional failures by finding the faith and the motivation to continue on
in spite of seemingly insurmountable obstacles. (In brief, Cayce's failures included: two photography studio fires, when he had worked as a
photographer and lost everything; being arrested for "practicing medi-
cine without a license"; failed speculation in oil wells; the death of an
infant son; years of being unable to find backing for his dream of an
Edgar Cayce hospital; losing the hospital only three years after it finally
became operational; and, recurring financial problems throughout his
life.)

In some respects, however, Cayce may have faced one of his ultimate
challenges in the form of Morton Blumenthal, one of his most influen-
tial supporters who, the readings suggest, had been none other than
Achilles—the very leader of the attacking army that had prompted Cayce
to kill himself in his lifetime as Xenon.

Interestingly enough, it was Edgar Cayce's experience with Morton
Blumenthal that he recalled more than a decade later when he was
dying. Actually, the break–up with Morton would trouble him for the
rest of his life. His own readings had pinpointed his incarnations in
Troy and in Egypt as periods when he and Morton had been antago-
nists. However, on his deathbed a "vision" of another experience in

which he had been together with Morton came to him as the source of the real problem that later erupted between the two men. According to Mae St. Clair (1908–2003; Mae Verhoeven at the time), who was a member of the office staff and a close friend of Edgar Cayce's, while in and out of consciousness Cayce recalled a past-life experience in Palestine when he had somehow taken advantage of Morton:

> . . . he roused himself to tell Mae Verhoeven, panting with the effort . . . his voice weak, that he had seen in a vision how he had mistreated the soul now Morton . . . [during] the rebuilding of Jerusalem after the Exile . . . Then his own arbitrariness and unkindness, he felt, had laid the groundwork for suspicion to develop suddenly between them centuries later in Virginia Beach—or so it seemed to him as suffering altered his consciousness and appeared to lift the veil of past-life memory. (Bro, pg. 345-346)

## Achilles: readings 900–6, 900–38, 900–63, 900–160, 900–261, 900–277, 900–334, 900–416, 900–426, 900–458

Morton Blumenthal and Edgar Cayce met through David Kahn, a mutual friend, in 1924. Morton was a young, handsome, extremely intelligent, wealthy, Jewish stockbroker who played a major role in Cayce's life and work. For the six years Morton was involved (1924–1930) all of Cayce's dreams for the future seemed possible, including the construction of Cayce's hospital where patients could come for readings and medical doctors, nurses, and therapists would carry out the treatment. Morton agreed to finance Cayce's hospital dream and made it possible for the Cayce family to move to Virginia Beach from Ohio.

Blumenthal's first reading, a health reading, had dealt, in part, with problems he was having with his tonsils. Thoroughly impressed with the accuracy and depth of the Cayce information, Morton would eventually have more readings from Edgar Cayce than any other individual—an astounding 468 over a period of six years! In addition to business, relationships, philosophy, education, and health, Blumenthal was also extremely interested in the subject of dream interpretation. In fact, 340 of Morton's 468 readings were on the subject of dreams.

Morton Blumenthal obtained his first life reading in October 1924. That reading suggested that Achilles had not simply been a mythological figure but had been a literal flesh–and–blood individual who had reincarnated in the present as Blumenthal himself. Perhaps hinting at the prospect that Morton would soon commit to underwriting Cayce's work in general and the hospital specifically, this self–certain, twenty–nine–year–old was also told that he was: "One upon whom many will rely for their mental activities in the Earth's forces. One that is given especially to being the control in many financial undertakings." (900–6)

Five months later, a follow–up reading would provide additional insights into the character of Achilles—a man, the readings said, who had been beloved by the common people for being a champion of individual freedom:

> **In the one before this, we find in that of Achilles in the Grecian or Trojan forces, and the entity then in that entity that has been proclaimed through many ages as the gifted one of the Gods, as understood by the people of that day, and one who became invincible to the destructive forces in earth's plane. Not through any condition of earthly existence. Rather the mental abilities to control those about the entity, for the entity gave the freedom to the common peoples, as known then, and brought much destructive forces to many, yet to the masses the greater love of the higher elements in a physical plane. In the personality as exhibited through the individuality at the present time, we find still that desire to be of help to each and everyone whom the entity contacts.** **900-38**

The following month, April 1925, Morton obtained a reading specifically on his lifetime as Achilles, asking for information on how he had developed or regressed during that period. The information stated that he had been born near Athens and had received all of the advantages of the day, enabling him to become a gifted warrior, and a man known for his physical and mental prowess. Because of the influence of his mother and because of coming in contact with various political figures of the day, he rose in stature and prominence among his own people:

> In the entrance into the earth's plane in that of, or called, Achilles, we find in the period of earthly existences when conditions were accentuated along certain lines. The entity then as the male offspring and entered in with the beauties of the rustic nature of the time and place, near Athenia or Athens, and raised to manhood, or young manhood, in and about the Mount, and given all advantages in the exercises and games and learning of the day, with the beauties of that in that day as could be obtained by one that was raised for the special purpose of entering into the political, social and other conditions of day and age. Soon learned that of the soldier with the spear, bow and axe, with an armor as prepared by the mother of the body, and given all the benefits of the aristocrats of the age, given exceptional abilities and applied same in the moral, physical, development of the body. One, then, beautiful of stature, physical, mind and of the expressing of same. Soon drawn in early manhood into the political situations surrounding the conditions of the country, coming then as a companion to many of the leaders in that day when there were personal combats in every phase of the physical prowess of the body. The entity showing the exceptional abilities of the environments under which the body had been developed in the day when this, the development of physical prowess, was studied and given the greater extent of attention. In personal combats often the body [was] successful and called the leader of the army and group, or the personal representative of the armies of the entity in the reign of those in charge of same at time.                                                                900-63

The reading went on to state that he had died after having been wounded in the heel, resulting in gangrene and blood poisoning. Regarding the question of how he had "regressed," or not lived up to his abilities, the reading pointed to the fact that it had not been necessary for him to die from that particular injury. Instead, he had erred by not choosing to quiet himself, be still, and enter into a state of consciousness in which he could have literally overcome his physical suffering and healed himself. With this in mind, the reading stated that in the present he needed to learn how to enter into this peaceful state of mind and overcome situations that otherwise would "overwhelm the entity." Cayce's advice as the reading came to a close was simply to: "Be still— and listen to the voice from within." (900–63)

That same year, Morton Blumenthal had a dream in which he apparently became conscious of the fact, while dreaming, that he was the sum total of all of his previous incarnations, including Achilles. The dream included a Voice that told him that he had been specifically born in the present to come to an understanding of how life works:

> **Then I saw the baby in the window for public display, the large eyes staring into space. I was walking and explaining to others at the same time and as I explained: I said: "I'm sort of confused now as to just who and what is really 'Me.' Now I was and still must be Achilles." I saw a tall, handsome, stalwart man in armor standing with spear in hand—it seemed 'Me.' "You see," I continued, "That is me and this is me and many others are Me."            900-160**

A second dream, in August 1926, encouraged him to draw upon his soul strengths as Achilles and to muster his energies, "not against the Trojans—but against ignorance, blindness, unconsciousness and death." A reading given on the dream suggested that it had been an effort to give him counsel and courage, "to throw self in that position of defense for a principle, even as Achilles, and the answer will be the courage, the leadership, the position, exercised by the present entity above them all." (900–261)

Extremely intelligent, Morton Blumenthal was one of few individuals among Cayce's contemporaries who could easily understand some of the most complicated concepts explored in the readings. According to his own life readings, because his soul had already accomplished a great deal in the physical/mental realms, his challenge in the present was to bring a new understanding of *oneness* and spirituality into the earth. In fact, Morton had been warned in a reading that unless he found a balance in life and his various activities, including the physical, the mental, and the spiritual, there would be a tendency for him to become unbalanced and even irrational (900–233).

A number of individuals who obtained readings from Edgar Cayce and had past-life experiences during the Trojan War were told of their connection to Achilles. For example, a thirty-four-year-old psychology professor was told that he had reported to Achilles and often gave the Greek hero personal counsel (204–1). On another occasion, a thirty-three-year-old medical doctor was informed that he had lost his life in defense of Achilles, apparently during the same battle in which Achilles himself had finally been killed (2739–1). Excerpts from each of their readings follow:

> In the one then before this we find in that period known as mythological, when there were wars among the Trojans—and the entity then among those that were in accord with those that would defeat the peoples gathered at the gate, and to Achilles did the entity report, and to him many were the counsels given and taken. In the name Tischol. The entity gained and lost through this experience. Gained through the application of self as respecting the interests of others. Lost through aggrandizing the power to which the entity arose; for while suffering may bring understanding, *causing* to suffer to satisfy one's own self brings reproach. Hence in the present experience there is ever the urge by the entity, to others and for self, Be True to Self in such a manner as to not bring reproach from others, and most of all from self.          204-1

> In the one before this we find in the period of the wars in that called the Trojan. The entity then among those who sought to aid in the routing when Achilles was brought low. The entity then losing the life in the defense of the household of that ruler or power. In that period in the name Arkimdor, and the entity lost and gained, and in the spirit of spite was the loss, in that of succor and aid the gain. In the urge as seen, that ability, determination, and ability for the entity to defy and carry out through mental forces

that as is right to the entity; yet is seen that conflicting again—
the entity will fight for right or wrong, whichever the entity is sided
with.
                                                                        2739-1

Morton Blumenthal, as mentioned earlier, was underwriting plans
for the Edgar Cayce hospital and would eventually create a short-lived
educational "Association of Learning" (Atlantic University), whose aspi-
ration was to acquaint individuals from all walks of life with an understanding of their soul nature and their relationship with God. The
following year a reading encouraged him to remain true to the purpose
for which he had incarnated in the present:

There has been placed, my son, in thine hands, again, that of position of the counselor to many peoples, and as there is gathered
about thee those who labored with and against thee—yet for that
one purpose as was to unify the knowledge that man in this mun-
dane sphere might have as respecting those Creative Forces as are
manifest in the material world . . .
                                                                        254-35

In 1926, a dream encouraged him to parallel information that he had
obtained in his past-life readings with written accounts regarding those
same periods in history. In a follow-up reading that discussed the
dream, Edgar Cayce told him that to discover more about his lifetime as
Achilles during the Trojan War, he should read Homer's *Iliad* (900–277).
Another dream the following year encouraged him to draw upon the
strength of Achilles in his business dealings when faced with personal
challenges that included ruthless people and their unscrupulous meth-
ods (900–334).

In a reading given in 1928, Edgar Cayce told Blumenthal that he
could achieve great physical, mental, and spiritual development in the
present by simply building upon two of his lifetimes from the past: a
counselor by the name of Aarat in ancient Egypt, and Achilles in Troy.
Cayce advised him: " . . . apply self in the way and manner as to merit
then that commendation of self, and the laudation of those that would
bring to the consciousness of self that knowledge, that understanding,

that in which others may know the truth and be free indeed." (900–416)
A few months later, another reading informed him that during his life–
time as Achilles, he had acquired the ability at a soul level to express in
the material world "strength that was not of an imposing character."
(900–426)

Finally, in October 1929, a reading advised Morton Blumenthal that
he possessed the ability to have such an incredible and lasting effect on
humanity's understanding of its relationship to God that the impact
would "resound much greater" than even the siege he had once led in
the taking of Troy (900–458).

That same year, the "Historical Committee" of Cayce's Association of
National Investigators, Inc., (precursor to the Association for Research
and Enlightenment, Inc.) compiled a number of past–life readings in an
effort to give various individuals additional insights into their present–
day relationships, taking into account the influence of past–life experi–
ences in which they had also encountered one another. Morton was
one of those individuals who received the report, simply called "His–
torical Data and Connections of Morton Blumenthal." The report in–
cluded the information that during previous incarnations in Egypt and
Troy, he and Edgar Cayce had been on opposing sides and in conten–
tion. In brief, the relationship advice outlined by the report included
the following information and suggestions:

> You [while in ancient Egypt] sided with the king [341] against the
> priest [(294)—Edgar Cayce] and there naturally arises from this
> a certain sense of disagreement from the point of principle rather
> than personal feelings . . . In the Trojan period [(294)—Edgar
> Cayce] was one of the guards of the gates of Troy. He was a stu-
> dent of chemistry by nature and one with considerable temper.
> There would naturally arise from this appearance a certain
> amount of antagonism since you were one of the leaders of the
> attacking forces.
>
> In the present this would take the form of signs of unreason-
> able temper in you both at times. Be careful of this and under-
> stand from whence it comes. Don't try to play Achilles [900] with

> **him for you will find him in moods just as stubborn as the Trojans who held out for seven [ten] long years.     900-275 Report File**

In spite of the above advice, less than eighteen months later Edgar Cayce and Morton Blumenthal parted ways. Blumenthal withdrew his funding from both Edgar Cayce and the hospital, forcing the hospital to close. Atlantic University would close a short time later. None of the promises of Morton's abilities to bring a new understanding to human-kind were ever realized, nor were Cayce's dreams for his own work ever fulfilled.

In part, the break between Edgar Cayce and Morton Blumenthal could be attributed to the financial strain of the stock market crash. However, there were additional contributing factors that may have been even more significant. One was the fact that Morton had a business falling-out with David Kahn, the individual who had first introduced him to Cayce. That falling-out led to legal claims and a lawsuit. Morton told Cayce not to give Kahn any more readings, but Cayce refused—partly because Kahn was a lifetime friend, partly because Cayce was not willing to let anyone tell him to whom he could give readings. Another factor was that one of the switchboard operators in Blumenthal's office began to show her own aptitude for giving psychic readings, and she and Morton began a very close relationship. Morton obtained readings from her whenever Cayce wasn't available, as well as using her to "check out" what was occurring in Virginia Beach. The switchboard operator's and Cayce's readings did not always agree with one another, and Morton became suspicious of Cayce's loyalty.

In the split that finally occurred, Morton stopped funding the hospital, the doors had to be closed, and Edgar Cayce's lifelong dream was lost. Cayce became depressed to the depths of his soul and, for a time, simply wanted to die. It was only months later when a meeting of Cayce's friends and supporters was held that ideas for a new organization sprang forth, and the Association for Research and Enlightenment, Inc., was formed

Demonstrating how souls tend to incarnate in groups, Morton had married a young woman whom the readings pinpointed as being none other than Helen of Troy reincarnated. The two would have their own share of difficulties, in part because of the innate traits and subconscious experiences that remained at a soul level from their respective experiences during the Trojan period.

## Helen of Troy: reading 136–1

In March 1925, Morton Blumenthal obtained a life reading for his twenty–year–old girlfriend, Adeline, whom he would marry three months later. The reading described her as being sentimental and stated that matters of love were extremely important to her. In addition to her soul strengths, which included a love of home and family, she was advised to work through two inclinations that remained with her at a soul level: one was the tendency to hold a grudge and the other was a pre-disposition "to get even" when angered. Her reading described her incarnations as including that of a musician in ancient Egypt, as well as being Helen of Troy:

> **In the one before this we find during the days when the Trojan forces were being attacked, the entity was in that capacity of one whom there was much made over, being in that of Helen of Troy. The entity then was in that development in the higher forces as found in physical body, development in mind, development in the law of love. In the present earth's plane we find the abilities to bring about self those who seek to give the acknowledgement of the abilities of the entity to fascinate many. Not in the manner of the one seeking those of the nature, yet the innate ability to bring these conditions; yet never lording them over any.                136-1**

The reading encouraged her to direct her energies into the building of a home "on a firm foundation" and the raising of a family. Although she had not known her soon–to–be–husband in Troy, he had known her from afar. The two had also been together in Egypt. Because she had a soul tendency to wish to dominate those around her, she was advised to seek harmony in her relationships with others.

When the "Historical Committee" of Cayce's Association of National

Investigators compiled Adeline's report on her past-life experiences and their influence on present-day relationships, the information and suggestions included the following:

> In that period [her Egyptian incarnation] as companion and pupil the entity learned to love and honor this man [(900)—Morton Blumenthal], and in the present the urge is easily seen . . . Then he appeared in the Troy period as Achilles, and led his Myrmidons against the city, fighting not so much to free Helen, as to gain glory and greatness for himself. He was shot in the heel, his one vulnerable point; and so far as we can discover never contacted with Helen, though holding her as the ideal for which he fought (same as "Make world safe for democracy"), and in present will fight for her and hold her as the ideal. Yet because of her he lost and was killed, and he may at times feel an unconscious or subconscious urge that the beauty and power of such a woman may be dangerous—but this is negligible, being dominated by many others. These two contacts are the only ones, and from them is seen the urges for a great love, a great companionship, and a great partnership for the good of all with whom these two contact.
>
> 136-82 Report File

During a reading given to a thirty-eight-year-old banker, Cayce stated that Achilles had gone out of his way to give much of himself to Helen, in spite of the fact that the two had never even met. The banker was told that he had been a warrior under Achilles and had been caught up in this very idea of defending Helen and home. At one point, he had also directed the taking of a city as part of the battle:

> In the one before this we find in that period known as the Trojan period. The entity then among those that aided in the defense under Achilles, and in that position defended the *home* and her [Helen of Troy (136)] whom Achilles gave much to and for. In the personal combats the entity, during that period, made for self a name among his peoples, and in the taking *of* the city when the

entity was sent by Achilles, when he withdrew, the entity gained possession, and cared for those whom the entity found favor in the physical favor of. In the name Ashtun. In the present these experiences bring for the entity much of that as is in defense of principle, in defense of other peoples' interest, in defense of state, in defense of home, in the defense of principle.                        1717-1

According to Morton Blumenthal, Adeline did not believe in reincarnation nor did she personally identify with her supposed connection with Helen of Troy. Nonetheless, Morton found the connection interesting when weighed against certain events that happened in Adeline's life:

She refuses to believe in reincarnation but things constantly happen to swing her back. For example, Mrs [ . . . ] brought her a book—*The Private Life of Helen of Troy*, by John Erskine—and one of the characteristics stressed therein is Helen's remaining unmoved during the trouble all about her, and that is Adeline's outstanding characteristic; her mother's sickness, her own trouble left her calm and collected; she just couldn't become rattled as did her sisters . . . As the Life Reading says [136-1], she can adjust herself to any condition . . . She just can't see herself as Helen of Troy . . . yet she does correlate certain characteristics in herself . . .                                      136-31 Report File

In April 1927, almost two years after the couple was married, Morton and Adeline had a son. At the age of one month, the boy would have a reading that stated he had given himself in service to Helen of Troy during the Trojan period:

Before this we find the entity was in that period when there were wars being made in that country now known as the Grecian. The entity then won in the defense of her taken as hostage for the followers of one who brought about the wars in that land.
Then in the name Ioniah, in the defense of principles, the entity

gained through that experience; being and becoming beloved by her whom the entity defended, and giving self in the service to same. Hence the urge as will be seen in the present experience will be that particular love shown for the mother [(136), Helen of Troy during Trojan period, now his mother], which is the urge seen through that experience.                                    142-1

For a time, things seemed to go relatively well for the family. Unfortunately, during the same period that Morton had his falling out with Cayce, the couple began to have their own marital problems, in part because of Morton's interest in the switchboard operator who was giving him readings. As a result, Adeline became extremely jealous and angry. In time, she sued for divorce and full custody of their son. Eventually, she would tell Cayce's secretary, Gladys Davis, that one of the reasons she had divorced her husband was because he had become "as a man who went off balance and was no longer a responsible person." (900-233)

After the divorce, Morton essentially disinherited his son and severed all ties between them. About the same time, he would lose the bulk of his finances and his seat on the New York Stock Exchange. He eventually supported himself by working in a printing firm. He died from a heart attack in 1954. Gladys Davis would eventually place the following notation in Adeline's file:

Who knows but what if [(136)—Adeline] had stuck with [(900)—Morton] regardless of his interest in [(3734)—the switchboard operator] and apparent off-balance activities, instead of giving way to the urge to "get even" as warned in 136-1, conditions might have turned out differently?                       136-83 Report File

## Hector: reading 5717-5

Arthur Lammers was a wealthy printer from Dayton, Ohio, who had an insatiable interest in the mystery religions, metaphysics, and psychic phenomena. It was one of Lammers's readings that opened up Cayce's interest in reincarnation. In October 1923, Lammers requested a horoscope reading for himself; at the end of which, Cayce uttered the curious statement, "He was once a monk." (5717-1) From that day forward, Cayce's work expanded beyond the physical readings for which he had gained recognition.

Lammers became so interested in Edgar Cayce's work that he offered to finance the Cayce family's move from Alabama to Dayton and to obtain readings to help cover living expenses so that Cayce could give readings full-time. At the time, Cayce ran a photography studio in Selma and gave readings part time. Lammers convinced him that he should abandon the photography business. In Dayton, Lammers was certain, Cayce's gift would find a willing audience.

Because Lammers was the first person to specifically obtain information on past lives[7], the readings provided only sketchy details, and none of those involved at the time ever obtained additional information. In Lammers's first reading when soul inclinations rather than specifically named incarnations had been sought, the readings suggested two tendencies that appear especially interesting, considering what the readings later said about Hector: "One that we find will bring destructive forces through its own appetites unless governed by the will forces of the soul portion of the individual"; and, "One whose forte lies in control of men." (5717-1) A follow-up reading added, "this body might become irrational in its actions . . . " (5717-2)

In 1930, a forty-three-year-old housewife received a life reading in which she learned that she had been a member of Hector's household. Rather than associating with his cruelty and tyranny, however, she had instead become a student and teacher of the philosophy that it was possible to learn to love and appreciate the beauty of all Creation:

> **In the one before this we find during that period known as the Trojan period. In that experience the entity was among those who were of the household of the one causing so much dissension among a peoples that were given to laud that of desire and of expressions**

---

[7]Gladys Davis later noted that information on past lives had been volunteered by the readings as early as 1911 but no one recognized it as such for decades (4841-1).

of beauty in every form. The entity *gained* through this experience, for the entity chose to teach—rather the concepts of that as
was given by the teachers of that period. In the name Momon. In
this experience those same teachings are *innate* in the entity's
inmost being, for beauty of form; beauty of mind, nobleness of
spirit, wonderfulness of expression, are worshipped even within—
but in accord with those of the *creative* forces.                    238-2

Suggesting that the war and perhaps Hector's negative influence had
spread beyond Troy for awhile, a reading for a twenty-three-year-old
stenographer in 1930 indicated that she had been among the island
people that had suffered at the time:

In the one before this we find in that period known as the Trojan,
and in this experience the entity was among those in the islands
that suffered under the overrunning of the country. While the entity only experienced a short life, or run, in this period—yet abun-
dant, and fraught much with the change in material *and* thought
of the day. In the name Iiliat. In the experience the entity gained,
yet much of grudge, much of that thought as of those in power
taking advantage—rather than the considering of *why* those were
*in* power. In the present there is held a peculiar influence as related to those of the opposite sex, and the mistrusts and the conditions of question arise much from *this* experience.                    1913-1

It was in November 1923 that Lammers' identity as Hector was finally mentioned when a reading was sought to discover the past-life
connections between Lammers, Cayce, Linden Shroyer, an accountant
and personal secretary, and a construction engineer by the name of
George Klingensmith. It was this reading that Cayce referred to when
telling Gladys Davis that the four of them had been brought together in
the hopes of learning to work constructively together, overcoming their
"destructive purposes" from the Trojan period. The reading briefly described their activities at the time of the Trojan War as follows: " . . .
[Lammers] as Hector, [Klingensmith] was in charge of the main gate, and

these of Cayce as that of warrior, and [Shroyer] as guard, you see. In this their destructive forces were shown for many ages . . . " (5717-5)

True to his word, Lammers financed the Cayce family move. Unfortunately, shortly after their arrival, the Cayces found Lammers completely entangled with problems in his business, including a lawsuit that took most of his time and energy. Almost immediately, Lammers was forced to declare bankruptcy, and the Cayce family saw their benefactor's finances dry up almost as quickly as they had appeared. It wasn't long before Lammers moved out of town. According to notes on file, Klingensmith and Shroyer would later report that Lammers had taken advantage of them as well—apparently demonstrating that some of the tendencies that had been attributed to Hector by the Cayce readings remained with Lammers at a soul level.

Because of the cyclic nature of reincarnation and the Cayce premise that every relationship must eventually be healed, it is apparent that these individuals will one day be brought back together. In that process they will inevitably encounter their own strengths and weaknesses in their relationships with one another.

To be sure, apart from the Edgar Cayce information on Troy that corresponds with historical and archaeological data, there is no way to verify much of this information. Still, it does not require unwavering belief; however, because so much of Cayce's other material has been verified since his death, this information certainly demands further inquiry.

# 7

# THE ARCHETYPAL SIGNIFICANCE OF THE TROJAN MYTH

Oftentimes mythic tales become classics for generations to come because they embody universal patterns of human experience that remain important to individuals regardless of the passage of time. Apart from the historical accuracy of such stories, these patterns can resonate to feelings, desires, experiences, fears, hopes, and dreams that are significant to the human condition. These mythic tales and legends often provide a mirror image of something similar occurring within the life experience of countless individuals, becoming personally relevant to them in the process.

First identified by Carl Gustav Jung (1875–1961), founder of the analytical school of psychology, these universal symbols or archetypes have meaning across time and cultures. They somehow encapsulate timeless patterns of human behavior and experience that have been frequently depicted in both life and the arts. For example, the archetype of the hero is portrayed in Homer's depiction of Hector and his dedication to home, family, and country above even his own desires. The same might be said of Virgil's depiction of Aeneas, who forsook his feelings for Queen Dido in the face of duty. The archetype of a tragic starcrossed love affair between opposites, such as that found in the *Tragedy of Romeo and Juliet,* can be pointed to in the relationship between Polyxena and Achilles. For every possible human condition there is a corresponding archetype.

Most often these correlations between patterns of human behavior and the archetypes that depict them occur not by design but because these universal patterns of human experience exist deep within the subconscious realms of the mind—the very realm from which imagination, storytelling, legend, and even divine inspiration spring. Although unintentional, whenever an author captures or describes an archetype for his or her audience, the work has the potential to become a classic. For example, at one level the wanderings of both Odysseus and Aeneas can correspond to Dorothy in the *Wizard of Oz* in her journey along the yellow brick road, each depicting the archetype of the soul's journey. This journey is the journey of life and entails adventures and experiences that eventually transform individuals to become who and what they were truly meant to be.

Mythic tales like the Trojan War often arouse something deep within the human psyche, capturing the imagination of countless people and generations to come. Because the story of the beleaguered Trojans and the depiction of the Trojan War in the *Iliad,* the *Odyssey,* and the *Aeneid* illustrate numerous archetypal patterns that are relevant even today, they remain classics. Although by no means exhausting all the universal symbols that can be found in Homer and Virgil, what follows are some of the most clearly evident patterns:

In the Trojan Myth, Troy held out against the much larger armies of Greece for an amazing ten years. With this in mind, there may be no greater symbol of nearly unbeatable defense than the Trojan army. It is for that reason that even a casual search of the Internet will reveal literally thousands of sports teams throughout North America that call themselves "the Trojans." In the twenty-first century, Trojan teams include every imaginable sport: football, soccer, basketball, baseball, archery, swimming, and even badminton, bowling, and golf. There are also Trojan stadiums and Trojan fields. (The same rationale of personal defense applies to the condom manufacturer who has adopted the name "Trojan" as its trademark.) All this bears witness to the fact that the best defense you can have is a Trojan.

At an archetypal level, we might imagine that Alexander the Great took the story of the *Iliad* with him on his military campaigns for several reasons. In part, the tale presents the age of heroes, men who are larger than life, and individuals who are willing to give even their lives for duty and country. From the Greek perspective, the story also symbolizes ultimate victory even in the face of the worthiest opponent. For both sides it depicts perseverance in the face of continuous obstacles. In addition, the argument between Achilles and Agamemnon might be read as the reconciliation of parts of the self. In other words, both men were warriors on the same side, and ultimately, apart from personal interests, each had the same goal; however, something prevented them from achieving their desired result. With this in mind, at an archetypal level the story suggests that personal integration becomes a necessary part of accomplishing any goal or overcoming any obstacle. In fact, at a subconscious level it demonstrates that the negative human emotions of pride, anger, lust, selfishness, and so forth must be brought under control by the self in order to fulfill the purpose for which an individual was born.

As already stated the *Odyssey* presents the archetype of the soul's journey. Many of Odysseus' wanderings can also correspond to universal patterns of human experience. For example, the land of the Lotus-eaters, whose food caused individuals to forget their true homes and wish to remain in that country, can represent the process of the soul coming into the earth and wishing to remain there, inadvertently forgetting all about its spiritual origins. Odysseus' own journey is one of perseverance—as is that of Penelope who waits for him for twenty years. At various parts in the tale, the reader can identify such patterns of the human condition as loyalty, hospitality, friendship, and—through the activities of the warrior Nestor—the wisdom that comes with age. Every bit as important, through the activities of Odysseus' son, Telemachus, we are presented with the story of a young man's coming of age—moving beyond the shadow of his parents and becoming a man in his own right.

In addition to depicting the soul's journey, the *Aeneid* demonstrates the pattern of how even the most brutally beaten underdog has the potential to become victorious. From a symbolic level, it is a tale that is meant to give inspiration to those who find themselves overcome with the events of the external world. This same archetype is illustrated in the life of Mahatma Gandhi, the true story of the racehorse Seabiscuit, and the Old Testament tale of Joseph, son of Jacob, who rises from the depths of prison and slavery to become second-in-command of all of Egypt. The *Aeneid* follows the adventures of the beleaguered and fleeing Trojans from total defeat and near annihilation to ultimate victory as the rulers of the known world, the Roman Empire. It is the ultimate tale of the vanquished becoming the victorious.

The Trojan Myth also provides us with a variety of characters who demonstrate a number of archetypal patterns through their actions, emotions, and experiences in the tale. As an example, Achilles has become one of the most memorable heroes of all time. It matters not that he is a flawed hero, who, for a time, places his feelings and ego above the call of duty. Eventually, because of the death of his friend Patroklos, he is transformed into an unbeatable warrior. Rather than detracting from his character, his flaws simply bring him closer to his human side, making it seem possible for others to attain to the same level of heroism. Once angry and vengeful, he learns to swallow his pride. He reconciles with Agamemnon, making his personal desires subservient to the greater good. He is a hero-in-progress.

To be sure, the symbol of Achilles' heel has become a well-known pattern of the human condition in its own right. At the most obvious level, it represents the fact that all individuals possess a fatal flaw or weakness that can overcome even the most invulnerable in appearance. At another level, the symbol of a heel can represent an individual's life direction. Thus, much like Achilles, we ourselves can become vulnerable by the choices we make and the directions we take in life.

The character of Homer's Hector provides us with the symbol of another type of hero—one that is less flawed and perhaps harder to emulate. In some respects, Hector is the ideal husband, father, brother, and leader. He places the needs of all others above his own. Whereas Achilles may be seen as being more prone to emotional extremes and personal feelings, Hector is stable, balanced, and unwavering in his commitment to his ideals. One reason the story is a tragedy is because the qualities of nobility, kindness, loyalty, and honor—as depicted in the character of Hector—are overcome by the very human emotions of anger and aggression, and the all-too-common experience of war.

In some respects the battle for Helen of Troy is symbolic of the desire and ultimate struggle for the perfect love that all humanity seeks. Helen is the archetype of the ideal woman—she alone is closest to the ideals of love and beauty as personified in the goddess Aphrodite. She is "the face that launch'd a thousand ships." Whether depicted in Helen's former suitors who take the Oath of Tyndareus, the actions of the entire armies of Greece and Troy, or the determination of Menelaus in reconciling with her even after twenty years, the love of Helen is a love worth fighting for.

Much like the story of Telemachus, the story of Paris can also be read as a tale of coming of age. It is the story of a child moving beyond the protection of parents and home and being forced by external events to begin a life on his or her own. Greek mythology suggests that before the Trojan War started, Paris lived in an idyllic realm. He was a simple shepherd with few cares, who was loved by and married to the nymph Œnone. In the same manner, the story of Adam and Eve, living in paradise and having few worries before eating the apple of temptation and experiencing "the Fall," can be viewed as this same kind of archetype. In the case of Paris, however, the apple of temptation was the golden apple of discord and having to choose "the Fairest" from among Hera, Aphrodite, and Athena. The choice he made led to his own "fall"—from the simple life he had once led on Mount Ida to becoming a central character in the conflict.

In part, each of the three goddesses that presented themselves to Paris can represent an aspect of humankind. Assuming that all individuals are composed of physical, mental, and spiritual components, each goddess can easily correspond to one of these three characteristics. For example, Athena is associated with wisdom and the intellect—some Greek legends even suggest that she sprang forth from the head of Zeus. For that reason, she represents the mental part or the mind of Paris. Conversely, Hera, as the sister to Zeus and queen of the gods, can aptly represent the spiritual component of this Trojan prince. Finally, Aphrodite with her physical beauty can be associated with his physical desires. Therefore, the story suggests that Paris "fell" from his paradise once he reached sexual maturity—the point at which he was forced to go out on his own.

The Trojan horse has become a symbol of unknown danger. Similar to a computer virus that has even taken on the name "Trojan horse," it is a gift that appears intriguing but is best left unopened. It corresponds to a hidden experience or message that is all-too-dangerous. It has become an archetype for being wary of things unknown.

A number of stories contained within the Trojan Myth explore the death of innocence. For example, this death-of-innocence pattern of behavior is illustrated in the attempted sacrifice of Iphigenia, by her father Agamemnon. This pattern is consistent with the Old Testament tale of Abraham attempting to sacrifice his son Isaac. The death of innocence is also depicted when King Laomedon's daughter is chosen to become the sacrifice of Poseidon's sea monster. In the case of Agamemnon, note how the war began only after the attempted sacrifice of his daughter—suggesting that only after innocence was lost was war even a possibility.

Throughout the story we have frequent occasions when a son overthrows or threatens to surpass his father. For example, Zeus defeats his father Cronus, just as Cronus had done to his father before him. Hecuba had a dream that indicated her child (Paris) would be a son who would eventually cause the death of his father and the destruction of the entire Trojan city. The sisters of Fate predicted that the son of Thetis would surpass his father. Each of these presents the archetype of the passage of generations and the overthrow of the old order as a means of making room for the new.

In brief, the oracles of old can correspond to intuition, which we all possess; the intuition of Cassandra is an appropriate depiction of the intuitive hunch we ignore that later proves correct. The various activities of the gods and goddesses throughout the myth can be associated with the ongoing involvement of God's presence in all of Creation—understood and witnessed at whatever level we ourselves can best understand. The descent of Odysseus and Aeneas into the land of the dead in Hades might represent the experience of coming in contact with our own unconscious minds. The list of possible examples goes on and on.

Clearly, the story of the Trojan Myth illustrates numerous instances when the activities of characters and unfolding events portray universal patterns of human experience and emotion that will remain relevant for as long as there are human beings. We can see our own hopes, fears, desires, and dreams played out before our eyes. We can observe characters who have been reliving this myth for thousands of years going through some of the same things we ourselves have experienced in life. The Trojan Myth has remained memorable for countless generations and cultures because it clearly portrays something universal about the human condition. It is our story, set against the backdrop of another time and another place.

# AFTERWORD

After more than 3,000 years, the story of Achilles, Hector, Paris, Helen, and the rest still continues to fascinate and inspire individuals the world over. Despite the fact that for much of that time there was no proof of the city's existence, the lack of evidence did little to detract from the myth's popularity. Legend has it that even Julius Caesar remarked that the city's total disappearance was simply due to the fact that Troy's very ruins were totally obliterated. Ever since the myth came to be known, the story of the Trojan War has never passed from human awareness, and—ever since they came to be written—the tales of Homer and Virgil have never gone out of print.

From one perspective, it is remarkable that a place the size of Troy could ever become so notable in the course of human events. In fact, Michael Wood, in his book *In Search of the Trojan War*, put together for the British Broadcasting Company, described it as follows:

> In its heyday, this tiny hill was still only the equivalent of a walled palace. Later it would become the acropolis of the classical city of New Ilium, situated in one corner of a small provincial town in the Roman Empire. It was never a great success, a boom town; its theatre was only built to accommodate 6,000 spectators, and its population may perhaps be more accurately gauged by an inscription (third or second century B.C.?) which says that 3,000 people had to be fed at one of the city's public feasts. That at least gives us some idea of the scale of the real city which existed on this site. (Wood, pgs. 12-13)

Why would such a place as this ever inspire the world? And, why would it take the massive Greek army ten years to overcome such a tiny place? This second question was also posed by the Athenian general and Greek historian Thucydides (ca. 460–400 B.C.), who is sometimes credited with being the originator of scholarly history. He theorized that the only reason the war could have lasted for such a length of time was that the Greek forces must have been undersupplied and poorly funded, causing them to spend much of their time, energy, and resources growing crops and engaging in acts of piracy simply to feed, fund, and support the troops: "In short, if they had stuck to the siege, the capture of Troy would have cost them less time and less trouble." (Crawley, pg. 9) He also believed that the Trojan War was a historic event that had already begun to take on mythic elements in his lifetime:

> "What enabled Agamemnon to raise the armament was more, in my opinion, his superiority in strength, than the oaths of Tyndareus, which bound the Suitors to follow him . . . He had also a navy far stronger than his contemporaries, so that, in my opinion, fear was quite as strong an element as love in the formation of the confederate expedition." (Crawley, pg. 7)

Through the legends set down by history, later verified through the efforts of archaeologists, we now know that such a place as Troy really existed. Today, it is generally assumed that some kind of Trojan War between Troy and the ancestors of the ancient Greeks actually occurred, but even now no one can claim with certainty the initial reasons behind the war. It seems unlikely that the abduction of one woman could rally the forces of two countries and thousands of men for so many years. A more likely scenario is that the strategic placement of Troy near the Aegean Sea and the Dardanelle strait caused contention between two countries over trade rights, access through the waterway, or even military superiority. Perhaps, as suggested by Edgar Cayce, these two powers had long been looking for a reason to go to war, and the story of Helen simply provided a means for a conflict that had been brewing.

Historically the most precise dating for the Trojan War is found on a slab of marble called the Parian marble, which chronicles various events from the ancient world dating back to the third century B.C. From this record, the destruction of Homer's Troy can be calculated to the day—June 5, 1209 B.C. Of course, legend maintains that the actual fall occurred in 1184 B.C. In any event, after the Trojan War, the site was abandoned until about 700 B.C. when Greek settlers occupied the area and renamed it Ilion. It was recaptured by the Romans around 85 B.C. but eventually lost importance, faded from memory, and became the stuff of legend.

What we can be certain of is that the entire story of Troy has yet to be revealed—even taking into account the information already gathered from legend, archaeology, history, and intuition. Perhaps it is no longer possible to discern all that occurred, why certain things happened, or even whether particular individuals really existed. But without a doubt, this ancient story will continue to capture the imagination, suggesting that not only may there be something more for us to learn about the Trojan Myth but that perhaps there is something the Trojan Myth can teach us about ourselves.

# Appendix A:
# Principal Characters in the Trojan Tale

**Acamas**  According to the *Aeneid*, he was one of the nine Greek captains who remained within the belly of the Trojan horse, waiting to attack the unsuspecting people of Troy.

**Acestes**  King of Drepanum, who was always hospitable to Aeneas and the surviving Trojans during their journeys, in part because his mother had been of Trojan descent.

**Achaemenides**  In the *Aeneid*, he was a surviving member of Odysseus's (Ulysses') crew who had been left behind at Sicily and was later picked up by Aeneas during his journeys. It was Achaemenides who warned Aeneas and the surviving Trojans about Polyphemus, the dangerous Cyclops.

**Achates**  The devoted friend and armor-bearer of Aeneas, who first entered the city of Carthage with him.

**Achilles**  Greek warrior, hero, and main character of the *Iliad*, he was considered one of the greatest warriors of all time. According to legend, he was the son of King Peleus of Athens and Thetis, a sea nymph. His withdrawal from the Greek–Trojan conflict because of a disagreement with Agamemnon over the fate of the captured girl, Briseis, is a central element of Homer's tale. Legend suggests that he was invulnerable with the exception of his heel by which his mother had held him when she dipped him in the River Styx. It was only after the death of his friend Patroklos that he healed his relationship with Agamemnon and reentered the war. He killed the Trojan Prince Hector. See also Appendix B, Cayce reading 900–6.

**Adrestus**

A Trojan warrior who was captured by the Greeks Menelaus and Agamemnon. In the *Odyssey*, he begged Menelaus for his life but was killed nonetheless because of the influence of Agamemnon.

**Aeneas**

According to legend, he was the son of the goddess Aphrodite and the Trojan Anchises. A warrior and member of the Trojan nobility, he was second-in-command to the Trojan prince, Hector. He and a group of Trojans survived the war and, according to Virgil's *Aeneid*, would journey to Italy where their descendants would establish the Roman Empire. At one point in his journey, he fell in love with Queen Dido of Carthage but was forced to forsake his love for her in pursuit of his duty. His first wife Creusa was killed during the Trojan War. His second wife Lavinia would give him the son Silvius, who would found the city of Alba Longa and become the ancestor of the Roman Empire.

**Aeolus**                Roman god of the winds who was influenced
                         by Juno (Hera) to bring fierce windstorms to
                         Aeneas and his fleet of surviving Trojans.

**Agamemnon**            Greek warrior, king, and the chief commander
                         of the Greek forces. His sister–in–law was
                         Helen of Troy, who was married to his brother
                         Menelaus from whom the Trojan prince, Paris,
                         had kidnapped her. In spite of being on the
                         same side, he had a rivalry with Achilles,
                         which is one of the main story lines in
                         Homer's *Iliad*. On his return from the war his
                         wife Clytemnestra murdered both him and
                         his Trojan concubine Cassandra.

**Aigisthos**            Lover to Clytemnestra, he usurped the throne
                         of King Agamemnon while the king was away
                         fighting the Trojan War. He eventually con-
                         spired with Clytemnestra, and the couple had
                         Agamemnon killed after his return at the end
                         of the war.

**Ajax**                 Considered one of Greece's greatest warriors.
                         During one portion of the Trojan War, he was
                         equally matched in hand–to–hand combat
                         with the Trojan warrior Hector. He eventually
                         fought Odysseus for the armor of the slain
                         Achilles and killed himself after it was
                         awarded to Odysseus. He is also called
                         Telamonian Ajax.

**Amor**            See Cupid.

**Anchises**        The father of Aeneas, he fled the burning city
                    of Troy with his son and his grandson
                    Ascanius. According to legend, Aeneas put his
                    father on his own back and carried him out
                    of the city. In the *Aeneid*, it was Anchises who
                    mistook the advice of the Oracle of Apollo to
                    continue on the journey to their true ances-
                    tral home to mean Crete rather than Italy. He
                    died during Aeneas' journey on the coast of
                    Sicily. While a spirit in the Elysium, he
                    showed his son the souls of future Romans
                    destined to be reincarnated and bring glory
                    to the future of Italy: Romulus, Caesar, Brutus,
                    Augustus Caesar, and others.

**Andromache**      Wife to the Trojan hero Hector and mother to
                    the infant Astyanax. According to some leg-
                    ends, after the death of her husband, she mar-
                    ried Hector's brother Helenus, oracle and seer,
                    with whom she established a small kingdom,
                    where Aeneas would later visit. Other legends
                    suggest that she had been forced to marry
                    Neoptolemus, the son of Achilles.

**Antenor**         Trojan nobleman who suggested after one of
                    the truces between the armies of Greece and
                    Troy that fighting could be stopped once and
                    for all simply by returning Helen to the
                    Greeks.

| | |
|---|---|
| **Antinous** | One of the most determined of Penelope's unwanted suitors, who pursued the woman during Odysseus' wanderings. |
| **Aphrodite (Venus)** | A daughter of Zeus, she was the goddess of love. According to Homer, she granted Helen to Prince Paris of Troy, resulting in the beginning of the Trojan War. Throughout the Greek–Trojan conflict she fought on the side of Troy, on one occasion rescuing Paris and, on another, her son, Aeneas. In Virgil's *Aeneid*, she stopped Aeneas from killing Helen and encouraged him to save himself and his family from the doomed city. Later, she told her son about Queen Dido and the city of Carthage and encouraged the two to fall in love. |
| **Apollo (Apollo/Phoebus)** | God of prophecy who once wooed and was rejected by Cassandra. In the Greek–Trojan conflict, he often intervened on the side of the Trojans. It was Apollo who forced the return of the maiden Chryseis by Agamemnon. It was Apollo who smote Patroklos when the Greek warrior was overpowering the Trojans; and, it was Apollo who whisked Aeneas to safety when the Trojan (and future ancestor of Rome) was on the verge of being killed. According to legend, Apollo was the god who expertly guided Paris's arrow into the heel of Achilles, causing a fatal wound. |

**Ares
(Mars)**

According to Homer, Ares helped the Trojans by coming to the aid of Hector and helping the warrior inspire his forces.

**Artemis
(Diana)**

Goddess responsible for the pestilence and the lack of winds visited upon King Agamemnon and his forces in response to Agamemnon's killing a deer that was sacred to her.

**Ascanius**

The son of Aeneas, he fled the burning city of Troy along with his father and Aeneas' father Anchises. In the *Aeneid*, it was Ascanius who inadvertently started the war between the Trojans and the Latins when he killed a pet stag that belonged to the daughter of King Latinus's herdsman.

**Astyanax**

Infant son of Hector and Andromache, who was killed during the siege of Troy by being thrown to his death from the city walls.

**Athena
(Minerva)**

A daughter of Zeus, she was the goddess of wisdom. According to Homer, throughout the Trojan War, she often aligned herself with the Greeks instead of the Trojans because of her hatred of Paris, who chose the goddess Aphrodite instead of herself as "the fairest." In spite of her support of the Greeks, however, she was responsible for Odysseus's wanderings at the end of the war.

| | |
|---|---|
| **Briseis** | Maiden captured by the Greek forces and awarded to Achilles after a raid on a neighboring town. Eventually, King Agamemnon claimed the girl as his own, resulting in Achilles feeling disrespected and withdrawing himself and his troops from the battlefront. |
| **Calypso** | Goddess who held Odysseus as her lover-captive for seven years after the Trojan War. |
| **Camilla** | According to legend, she was a mighty, virgin warrior who came to the aid of the Latins during their battle with Aeneas. In the end, she was killed by the Trojans. |
| **Cassandra** | Daughter of King Priam and Queen Hecuba of Troy. She was wooed by the god Apollo, who granted her the gift of prophecy. However, because the romance did not work out, Apollo caused all of her prophecies to be ignored. After the war she was abducted by the Greek King Agamemnon to be his concubine but was eventually murdered by his wife, Clytemnestra. |
| **Chiron** | A centaur (half man and half horse) who was responsible for training Achilles to become one of the greatest warriors of all time. |
| **Chryseis** | Maiden captured by the Greek forces and awarded to King Agamemnon after a raid on a neighboring town. After the king was forced |

to return her to the girl's father because of the intervention of the god Apollo, Agamemnon claimed the maiden Briseis in exchange, resulting in an argument with Achilles and Achilles withdrawal from the war.

**Clytemnestra**     Wife to King Agamemnon, sister to Helen, and mother to Iphigenia. While her husband was gone fighting the war for so many years, she became the lover and companion of Aigisthos. In spite of her own infidelity, she murdered her husband and his lover Cassandra after the Greek–Trojan conflict had come to an end.

**Creusa**     Wife of Aeneas, who was inadvertently left behind when Aeneas fled the burning city of Troy with their son Ascanius and Aeneas' father Anchises. She perished in the battle and returned as a ghost to encourage her husband to seek out a new Troy where he would find a new wife.

**Cupid (Amor)**     God of love. In the *Aeneid*, the god influenced Queen Dido to fall in love with Aeneas.

**Cyclops**     See Polyphemus.

**Demodocus**     Blind minstrel in the kingdom of Phaeacia who sang about the fall of Troy in front of Odysseus and an assembly.

**Diana**          See Artemis.

**Dido**           Queen of Carthage, who fell madly in love with Aeneas, forsaking her duties in the process. Originally from Tyre, she and her people had immigrated to the coast after the death of her husband. After she was abandoned by Aeneas, she committed suicide and snubbed him when they later met in Hades.

**Diomedes**       One of the most heroic Greek warriors, known for his skill and bravery. He dedicated himself to the Greek troops and held himself apart from personal biases and arguments. He and Odysseus reportedly disguised themselves and sneaked into Troy, as a means of stealing the Palladium—a statue of Athena—from her temple. At one point in the *Iliad*, Diomedes demonstrated that peace between Troy and Greece was possible because he and the Trojan Glaukos reconciled when it was discovered that their ancestors had been friends. From Homer's depiction, his dedication to duty and honor on the Greek side was similar to Hector's commitment to the Trojans.

**Dolon**          Trojan spy who was sent to the Greek camp and was captured by Odysseus and Diomedes, and eventually killed by Diomedes.

**Epeios**

According to legend, Epeios was the actual architect of the Trojan horse, which Odysseus filled with Greek fighters and took into Troy. According to the *Aeneid,* he was also called the "master builder," and he was one of the nine Greek captains who remained within the belly of the Trojan horse, waiting to attack the unsuspecting people of Troy. See also Appendix B, Cayce reading 470-2.

**Eris**

Goddess of discord. She was responsible for bringing the famed golden apple that was labeled "To the Fairest" to the wedding of Thetis and Peleus. The apple caused the disagreement between Aphrodite, Athena, and Hera and contributed to the immortals' lengthy involvement in the Trojan War.

**Evander**

Father of Pallas and king of the small town of Pallanteum. He formed an alliance with Aeneas in the Trojans' battle with the Latins.

**Ganymede**

Young male Trojan who was appointed by Jupiter (Zeus) to be the eternal cup-bearer and wine-pourer for the gods, greatly upsetting Juno (Hera) in the process.

**Glaukos**

Trojan warrior who stopped fighting with the Greek warrior Diomedes once the two discovered that their ancestors had been friends.

| | |
|---|---|
| **Hector** | Son of King Priam and Queen Hecuba of Troy, and therefore a Trojan prince and commander of the Trojan forces. He was the brother to Paris. In Homer's account he held honor and family above all else, and was courageous and put the needs of Troy ahead of his own desires. During one portion of the Trojan War, he was equally matched in hand-to-hand combat with the Greek warrior Ajax. According to legend, he killed Achilles's best friend, Patroklos, inadvertently causing Achilles to reenter the war and resulting in Hector's own death. In the *Aeneid*, it was the ghost of Hector who came to Aeneas in a dream to worn him what was befalling the city of Troy, thereby allowing Aeneas' escape. See also Appendix B, Cayce reading 5717-5. |
| **Hecuba** | Queen of Troy and wife of King Priam, she was the mother of the Trojan heroes, Paris and Hector, as well as the prophetess Cassandra. After the Trojan War she was taken prisoner by the Greeks. |
| **Helen** | According to legend, she was the daughter of Zeus, who had seduced her mother, Leda (the wife of Tyndareus), in the guise of a swan. Her beauty was legendary, causing her to be wooed by nearly every Greek warrior and king. Married to King Menelaus of Sparta; according to Homer her abduction by the Trojan prince, Paris, was the initial cause of |

the Greek–Trojan conflict. See also Appendix B, Cayce reading 136–1.

**Helenus**

A Trojan seer and oracle who was a brother to Hector. According to some legends, after the Trojan War, he married his brother's widow, Andromache, and the two established a small kingdom where Aeneas would later visit.

**Hephaestus (Vulcan)**

God of fire. Legend claims that Hephaestus was responsible for creating the armor for the Greek warriors Achilles and Odysseus, as well as the Trojan warrior Aeneas.

**Hera (Juno)**

Sister–wife to Zeus and queen of the gods. According to Homer, throughout the Trojan War, she aligned herself with the Greeks instead of the Trojans, in part because of her hatred of Paris, who chose Aphrodite instead of herself as "the fairest." Her hatred of the Greeks continued through Aeneas's journey to Italy, such as when she used the messenger goddess Iris to upset the surviving Trojan women and cause them to set fire to the Trojan vessels in retaliation for their husbands' years of wandering.

**Hermes (Mercury)**

Messenger god who took Protesilaus, first Greek killed at the start of the Trojan War, back to see his wife, Laodamia, for a three-hour conversation after the warrior's death. He also helped Odysseus escape from the isle of Calypso. In the *Aeneid*, Hermes was sent to Aeneas to remind him of his duty to found a new Troy, resulting in the Trojan having to leave Queen Dido at Carthage.

**Hermione**    The only daughter born to Menelaus, King of Sparta, and Helen of Troy. Some legends suggest that the girl married Neoptolemus, the only son of Achilles.

**Iphigenia**    Daughter of King Agamemnon and Queen Clytemnestra. She was to be used as a sacrifice to the goddess Artemis in response to her father having killed a sacred deer. Some legends suggest that she was saved from death, becoming a priestess in one of Artemis' temples.

**Iris**    Messenger goddess in the *Iliad* who warned Hector that Agamemnon and the Greek forces were preparing for battle. In the *Aeneid*, Iris was used by Hera (Juno) to upset the surviving Trojan women, causing them to set fire to the Trojan vessels in retaliation for their husbands' years of wandering.

**Juno**    See Hera.

**Jupiter/Jove**    See Zeus.

**Kalchas**    Greek soothsayer and oracle who was often relied upon by the Greek forces for advice, insights, prophecies, and information on the activities and whims of the gods.

**Laertes**          The father of Odysseus, he lived with Penelope and Telemachus during the many years that his son was away and wandering.

**Laocoön**          A Trojan priest who warned the people not to bring the Trojan horse inside the city gates by uttering the famous words, "even when Greeks bring gifts I fear them, gifts and all."

**Laodamia**         Wife of Protesilaus, first Greek killed at the start of the Trojan War. News of his death brought such sadness that she beseeched the gods and was allowed to have a three-hour meeting with her deceased husband.

**Latinus**          King of the Latins who promised the hand of his daughter Lavinia to Aeneas in fulfillment of an ancient prophecy.

**Lavinia**          Second wife of Aeneas and mother to their son, Silvius. According to legend, the city of Lavinium was named after her by Aeneas, the city's founder.

**Lycomedes**        It was to the kingdom of King Lycomedes that Thetis sent her son Achilles, disguised as a woman, as a means of avoiding the Greek–Trojan conflict after the Oath of Tyndareus had been invoked.

**Machaon**          According to the *Aeneid*, he was one of the
                     nine Greek captains who remained within the
                     belly of the Trojan horse, waiting to attack
                     the unsuspecting people of Troy.

**Mars**             See Ares.

**Memnon**           Ethiopian prince and ally to Troy. Legend
                     states that he was killed in hand–to–hand
                     combat with Achilles.

**Menelaus**         King of the Greek province of Sparta and
                     younger brother of Agamemnon. His wife,
                     Helen, was abducted by the Trojan prince,
                     Paris, resulting in the beginning of the Trojan
                     War. According to the *Aeneid*, he was one of
                     the nine Greek captains who remained within
                     the belly of the Trojan horse, waiting to at-
                     tack the unsuspecting people of Troy. After
                     the war, he and Helen were reunited and
                     spent the rest of their lives together. Legend
                     suggests that the couple had one daughter,
                     Hermione.

**Mercury**          See Hermes.

**Minerva**          See Athena.

**Neoptolemus**      The only son of Achilles. Some legends sug-
                     gest that after the war he married Hermione,
                     the daughter of Menelaus and Helen; others
                     suggest that he took Hector's widow,

Andromache, to be his wife. According to the *Aeneid*, he was one of the nine Greek captains who remained within the belly of the Trojan horse, waiting to attack the unsuspecting people of Troy. It was generally thought that he was the Greek who killed King Priam of Troy. In some legends, Neoptolemus was also called Pyrrhus.

**Neptune**            See Poseidon.

**Nestor**             Oldest and wisest warrior among the Greek forces. He tried to give wise counsel to both Agamemnon and Achilles and often encouraged Agamemnon to end the differences that existed between the two.

**Odysseus**           Greek warrior, hero, and king of Ithaca.
**(Ulysses)**          He served as adviser to Agamemnon and acted as a mediator between Agamemnon and Achilles. A member of the Greek forces in the *Iliad*, he became the central character and hero in the *Odyssey*. In Homer's epics he was portrayed as being brave and cunning, and it was to him that the armor of Achilles was awarded after the Greek hero's death. He and Diomedes stole the Palladium in an effort to win the war. Legend says that Odysseus also suggested the ploy of the Trojan horse. As had been prophesied before his entrance into war, he spent ten years fighting the Trojan War and another ten trying to return to his home

in Ithaca. According to the *Aeneid*, he was also called "the man of iron," and was one of the nine Greek captains who remained within the belly of the Trojan horse, waiting to attack the unsuspecting people of Troy.

**Œnone**
Beautiful nymph who loved and married Paris but was abandoned when he began his search for Helen.

**Oracle of Apollo**
In the *Aeneid*, the seer and oracle who encouraged the surviving Trojans to continue on the journey to their true ancestral home, which Anchises mistakenly interpreted to mean Crete rather than Italy.

**Palamedes**
King Agamemnon's messenger who delivered the call to arms after the Oath of Tyndareus had been invoked. He saw through Odysseus's ploy of feigning madness as a means of avoiding the conflict.

**Palinurus**
In the *Aeneid*, he was the Trojan navigator who lost his life in payment to Poseidon (Neptune) for insuring Aeneas and his remaining Trojans safe passage to Italy.

**Pallas**
Son of King Evander of Pallanteum, and ally to Aeneas during his battle with the Latins. He was eventually killed by Turnus, which prompted Aeneas to kill Turnus in return.

**Pandaros**        Trojan warrior who was influenced by the
                    goddess Athena to break one of the truces
                    between Greece and Troy by injuring
                    Menelaus with an arrow.

**Paris**           Trojan prince who was abandoned by his par-
                    ents, King Priam and Queen Hecuba of Troy,
                    because of a prophecy that he would bring
                    destruction to the city. A brother of the Tro-
                    jan hero Hector, according to legend he chose
                    Aphrodite as "the fairest" rather than Athena
                    or Hera, thereby causing the anger of the
                    other two. His kidnapping of Helen to be his
                    wife and concubine in spite of the fact that
                    she was already married to the Greek King
                    Menelaus is often recounted as the cause of
                    the Greek–Trojan conflict. According to leg-
                    end, he was responsible for the death of the
                    Greek hero Achilles. He was killed by
                    Philoctetes with the poison arrows of Hercules.

**Patroklos**       Greek warrior and squire and best friend of
                    Achilles. He acted as an intermediary between
                    the forces of Achilles and the rest of the Greek
                    army. He also borrowed Achilles' armor for
                    himself as a means of inspiring the Greeks
                    and striking fear into the hearts of the Tro-
                    jans. He was struck down by the god Apollo
                    and killed soon thereafter by Hector. His
                    death resulted in Achilles' reconciliation with
                    Agamemnon, as well as the warrior's return
                    to battle.

**Peleus**              King of Athens, husband to Thetis, and father of Achilles.

**Penelope**            Wife of Odysseus, cousin to Helen, and mother to Telemachus. A line of unwanted suitors wooed her during the twenty years that her husband's wanderings kept him from his home in Ithaca.

**Penthesilea**         Warrior–queen of the Amazons and an ally to Troy. She came to assist the Trojans during the war but was killed by Achilles.

**Philoctetes**         Greek warrior who was in possession of the fabled bow and arrows of Hercules. Just prior to the Trojan War, the Greeks abandoned him on an island because he had been wounded and the stench put off from his sore was over-powering. He was eventually healed of his condition and brought into the war with Hercules' bow and arrows, of which Paris became the first victim.

**Polydore**            Slain Trojan who was brutally murdered at the city of Thrace. From the grave he warned Aeneas to continue on the journey after the surviving Trojans had first arrived at the city.

**Polyphemus**          The Cyclops. One–eyed monster, who was a son of Poseidon. His main appearance was in the *Odyssey*, where he was outsmarted and blinded by Odysseus.

**Polyxena**

Daughter of King Priam and Queen Hecuba, she became infatuated with Achilles, just as he became infatuated with her. They were to have been married, but Achilles died at the hand of her brother, Paris. Legend states that she either killed herself or was sacrificed on Achilles' tomb.

**Poseidon (Neptune)**

God of the sea and brother to Zeus. He was also the father to Polyphemus, the one-eyed Cyclops. He became a longstanding enemy of the Trojans for their failure to pay him for his assistance in constructing the city's protective walls. In the *Aeneid*, however, he intervened on the side of the Trojans because he was upset that Juno (Hera) and Aeolus, the god of the winds, were trying to usurp his power. He also granted Aeneas and the remaining Trojans safe passage on their journey to Italy in exchange for one Trojan life: Palinurus, the ship's navigator.

**Priam**

King of Troy and husband of Queen Hecuba. The father of the Trojan princes Hector and Paris and the prophetess Cassandra, he was killed during the siege of Troy. Some legends suggest that the Greek warrior Neoptolemus, the only son of Achilles, killed him.

**Protesilaus**

First Greek killed at the beginning of the Trojan War. His death occurred the instant his foot touched Troy's shoreline. Some legends suggest that it was Hector who killed him. After his death, he was allowed a three-hour meeting with his grieving wife, Laodamia.

**Proteus**          Assistant to Poseidon who informed Menelaus that Odysseus had been held as lover and captive upon Calypso's island.

**Pyrrhus**          See Neoptolemus.

**Remus**          Twin brother to Romulus, who was born to the Vestal Virgin Ilia after her marriage to Mars. Nursed by a she-wolf after being discarded by his cruel stepfather, he and his brother are regarded as the legendary founders of Rome. He was killed by Romulus in a dispute over the city's borders.

**Romulus**          Twin brother to Remus, who was born to the Vestal Virgin Ilia after her marriage to Mars. Nursed by a she-wolf after being discarded by his cruel stepfather, he and his brother are regarded as the legendary founders of Rome. He killed Remus after a dispute over the city's borders, making himself the first leader of Rome in 753 B.C.

**Sibyl**          In the *Aeneid*, she was the priestess of Apollo who had been granted the gift of prophecy by Apollo. In addition to advising Aeneas about a final war he had to fight, she took him on an other-world journey in which he

visited Hades and the Elysium, where he perceived the souls of future Romans of note
waiting to be reborn.

**Silvius**      Son of Aeneas and Lavinia. He would found
the city of Alba Longa and from him would
come the ancestors of Rome.

**Sinon**       Greek warrior purposely left behind by
Ulysses (Odysseus) when making it appear
that the Greeks had abandoned the war. His
purpose was to lie to the Trojans, thereby
convincing them to allow the Trojan horse
into city. He also set free Ulysses and the other
Greeks from inside the belly of the Trojan
horse.

**Sthenelus**   According to the *Aeneid*, he was one of the
nine Greek captains who remained within the
belly of the Trojan horse, waiting to attack
the unsuspecting people of Troy.

**Telemachus**  Son of Odysseus and Penelope. When he
came of age, he went in search of his father,
in the process becoming a man in his own
right.

**Telephus**    King of Mysia who beat the Greek forces two
years after the abduction of Helen, when they
mistakenly landed at his kingdom thinking it
was Troy.

**Thessandrus**     According to the *Aeneid*, he was one of the nine Greek captains who remained within the belly of the Trojan horse, waiting to attack the unsuspecting people of Troy.

**Thetis**          Beautiful sea nymph who was once wooed by Zeus but instead married King Peleus of Athens. She and Peleus became the parents of Achilles. As an immortal, she was the frequent liaison between her son and Zeus. See also Appendix B, Cayce reading 302-1.

**Thoas**           According to the *Aeneid*, he was one of the nine Greek captains who remained within the belly of the Trojan horse, waiting to attack the unsuspecting people of Troy.

**Turnus**          Latin who was in love with Lavinia and became unhappy when she was promised to Aeneas. In the *Aeneid*, he was killed by Aeneas in the final battle before the surviving Trojans could settle in their new city.

**Tyndareus**       Early king of Sparta, husband to Leda and stepfather to Helen. Known for the Oath of Tyndareus, which united all of the Greek city-states as allies against the Trojans because of Paris's involvement in Helen's kidnapping.

**Ulysses**         See Odysseus.

**Venus**           See Aphrodite.

**Vulcan**         See Hephaestus.

**Zeus**           The supreme god of Olympus. Although
**(Jupiter/Jove)** he often tried to appear neutral throughout
                   the Trojan War, he generally allowed his sym-
                   pathies to be with the Trojans. In the *Aeneid*,
                   he predicted the eventual success of the sur-
                   viving Trojans in founding their new city.

# APPENDIX B:

# CAYCE READINGS AND THE TROJAN TALE

| Cayce reading number | Name (if given) and essential information provided for the individual about his or her past–life experience during the time of Troy. Sex, age, and occupation at the time of the reading (or first relevant reading, if more than one). Date of reading. |
|---|---|
| | *Please Note: When Edgar Cayce gave past-life information for an individual, he provided only that information that had a direct and important bearing on the present lifetime. This suggests that—out of all of the individuals who had Cayce readings—only these people were being affected by their Trojan War incarnations.* |
| 5–2 | Ashtubol. Tried to serve as a mediator between the Greek and Trojan forces. Male, 36, attorney. June 23, 1930. |
| 6–2 | Muriel. Trojan female who defended the city against the invading Greeks. Female, 33, social worker. June 21, 1930. |
| 99–6 | Hault. At various times served as the first and second guard at the Trojan gate. Male, 38, merchant. August 2, 1930. |
| 101–1 | Xenia. Although a female aid to Paris, she helped Achilles enter the city. Female, 51, osteopath. November 11, 1929. |

| | |
|---|---|
| **136–1** | Helen of Troy. She was beautiful in body and mind, and central to much of the overall conflict. She was married to Achilles (900) in the present. Female, 20, housewife. March 5, 1925. |
| **142–1** | Ioniah. Greek who served in defense of Helen of Troy. In the present he was the son of Helen (136) and Achilles (900). Male infant, one month old. May 15, 1927. |
| **204–1** | Tischol. Assistant to Achilles who often provided personal counsel. Male, 34, psychology professor. January 10, 1929. |
| **238–2** | Momon. Among the household of the Trojan rulers. Female, 43, housewife. February 13, 1930. |
| **259–8** | Garcia. Companion of the assistant gatekeeper. Her drawings of the city's gates and defenses apparently enabled Achilles's forces to overcome those who supported Hector. Female, 18, optometry student. September 4, 1934. |
| **294–8, 294–9, 294–19, 294–161 294–183** | Xenon. A Trojan student, chemist, sculptor, and artist. With the onslaught of the Greek Trojan conflict, he became a soldier and defender at the gate. He committed suicide when he failed to understand the conspiracy that enabled the Greeks to lay siege to the city. Male, 46, clairvoyant. February 9, 1924. |

| | |
|---|---|
| **302–1** | "In the flesh" mother of Achilles—no name given. Possessed the ability to rule and guide men; gave much strength and power to her son. Female, 36, saleswoman (who worked in [900]'s brokerage office). September 26, 1927. |
| **369–3** | Pamn. Among those who ministered to the guards at the gates to the city. Female, 22, college student. November 3, 1927. |
| **470–2** | Cajhalon. Greek individual who was the main architect/builder of the Trojan horse. Lost his life during the siege and burning of the city. Male, 35, construction engineer. May 15, 1925. |
| **568–1** | Ulan. One of those Greeks who worked out the plan for using the Trojan horse as the means of entering the city of Troy. Male, 20, occupation unknown. June 2, 1934. |
| **692–1** | Schulen (also called Hulen). Associated with the forces of Achilles; she brought art and literature to some of the people after the death of Hector. Female, 39, secretary. October 12, 1934. |
| **758–23** | No name given. One of the communicators stationed at the main exit to the city, helping to control those that entered and exited the city. Male, 8, retarded youth. November 4, 1930 |

**820–1**            Sheulen. A Greek soldier who took part in the wars upon the isles of Crete. Male, 25, government clerk. February 8, 1935.

**900–6, 900–38**    Achilles. Greek warrior and hero. According to
**900–63, 900–160,** Cayce readings, in spite of his ability to cause
**900–261, 900–277** great destruction, he was a hero of the com-
**900–334, 900–416,** mon people and was loved by Greeks and Tro-
**900–426, 900–458** jans alike. The readings suggest that Hector was a hated ruler and that many of the Trojans saw Achilles as their deliverer. He was married to Helen (136) in the present. Male, 29, stockbroker. October 14, 1924.

**957–1**            Phien. Trojan counselor who oversaw and supervised many of the warriors; he tried to serve as a mediator of peace between Achilles and Hector. Male, 53, philosophy professor. March 12, 1930.

**993–1**            Ialea. One of those who attempted to defend the Trojan gates when the Greek forces overran the city. Female, 39, occupation unknown. July 17, 1929.

**1082–3**           Sujon. Closely associated with a number of Achilles' leaders; she became disillusioned with some of those in authority because of their "wild" social activities. Female, 41, clothier and housewife. November 12, 1937.

**1225–2**           Smoniel. Part of the Trojan forces that defended the gates but took sides with Achilles and his forces in destroying Hector's influence. Male, 20, occupation unknown. September 17, 1932.

1717-1   Ashtun. One of the chief warriors under Achilles who was primarily responsible for the Greek defense. Male, 38, bank cashier. June 25, 1930.

1728-2   Saladbid. Trojan soldier who was part of the defense on the eastern gate to the city. Male, 42, salesman. August 23, 1930.

1730-1   Elois. Wife of one of the gatekeepers to the city of Troy; she was partially responsible for providing meals to some of the city's gatekeepers. Female, 25, dietician. August 29, 1930.

1739-8   No name given. One of those who lost their lives in defense of the Trojan wall and gate during the siege. Male, 36, furniture salesman. October 25, 1930.

1913-1   Iiliat. One of the island people who suffered during the overrunning of the country by Hector and his forces. Female, 23, stenographer. November 26, 1930.

1918-1   Helois. One of the Greek rulers who oversaw a small kingdom in the south of Greece during the beginning of the Trojan War. Female, 41, music teacher. December 11, 1930.

**2694–1**      Sansan. Individual who guided the small sailboat that carried Achilles to the shores of Troy. Male, 31, realtor. July 16, 1927.

**2738–1**      Odessa. Served as a messenger from Troy to the coastline. Male, 32, radio wholesaler manager. February 11, 1930.

**2739–1**      Arkimdor. Defender of Achilles who sought to aid the warrior after he was wounded. He lost his life in the struggle. Male, 33, doctor. December 29, 1926.

**2750–1**      Milio. Female Trojan warrior who assisted in watching the gate and defending the city. Female, 44, housewife. March 12, 1930.

**2813–1**      Rekulus. A maker of mechanical weapons for defense. Male, 45, bowling alley manager. September 12, 1942.

**2856–1**      Parsia. A Trojan who resented those in power and fell under the influence of Achilles. He took part in the Trojan horse deception. Male, 36, shirt manufacturer. June 7, 1930.

**2886–1**      No name given. A Trojan who was among the city's defending forces; however, he rose against Hector and his power in order to overthrow the Trojan ruler. Male, 32, commercial banker. May 7, 1929.

**2896–1**    Ioncolm. One of the defenders of the Trojan gate who settled in Crete and became a counselor after the Trojan War. Male, 22, journalist. May 2, 1930.

**2940–1**    No Name given. Trojan who attempted to live up to his ideals—physically, mentally, and spiritually. Male, 26, soldier. March 21, 1943. Reading excerpt not included elsewhere, as follows:

"First, as indicated—study self and self's purposes. Know thy ideals—spiritual, mental, material. Study to show self approved unto such ideals. For, as was demonstrated, as was testified of in thy activities in Rome, in Jerusalem, in Caesarea, in Troy, in Philippi—thine own body is the temple of the living God. There He has promised to meet thee." (2940–1)

**4121–2**    Ixnoz. Was in charge of the main gate during the period of the Trojan War. Although not Trojan by birth, he had apparently immigrated to the city. Male, 25, construction engineer. December 4, 1923.

**4180–1**    Thesiolups. A Trojan soldier and defender of the gates. Male, 26, occupation unknown. May 21, 1926.

**4198-3**        No name given. One of the guards under the
                  direction of Achilles who was later promoted
                  because of his loyalty. Male, 34, occupation
                  unknown. January 23, 1925. Reading excerpt
                  not included elsewhere, as follows:

                  "In the one before this, we find in the rule
                  when the Trojan Wars, and under the direc-
                  tion of Achilles. In this entity then, guard to
                  gates, and was that entity then that met Achil-
                  les in the time when that entity found
                  strength over physical enemies, and was then
                  raised up to high position, which the entity
                  afterward gave self to self-debasement."
                  (4198-3)

**4227-1**        No name given. A member of the Trojan
                  forces. Female, 35, housewife. Reading excerpt
                  not included elsewhere, as follows:

                  "Again in the Trojan forces, when the body,
                  through spiritual, mental, forces, suffered
                  much, but to the uplift of the forces as is set."
                  (4227-1)

**4898-1**        Aphori. Greek woman who was captured by
                  the Trojans and taken to Crete. Female, 17, oc-
                  cupation unknown. April 23, 1925.

**5453-3, 5453-4,**  Asarat. Assistant to the keeper of the gates; re-
**5453-5**        sponsible for barring some from entering the
                  city. Male, 25, accountant. November 20, 1923.

Reading excerpts not included elsewhere, as follows:

"Before this we find this body in the days of the Trojan wars. That of the assistant to the keeper of the gate, see? who barred the way to the entrance of those who would destroy the city, see?" (5453-3)

"In that previous [Troy], we find in the keeper in gate that as is shown in ability to be centered one objective, irrespective of what may be brought to bear upon the person in physical elemental forces, and the desire to do or to expend all of self in the making of that principle as set before self, whether good or bad." (5453-4)

"In the one before this we find in the guard at the gate [in Troy], then in that of Asarat, and the entity in the association in this time has had many associations, both for weal and woe, and will have many others of the same period in present life. The findings then in individuality and personality as exhibited in the present time come to those likes and dislikes that are in the individual's latent force, yet rarely expressed in the open." (5453-5)

**5454-3**  Abidouel. A musician who later became a soldier and defender of the Trojan gates. Male, 8, student. March 14, 1927.

**5540-5**        Ilhouead. One of Achilles' forces; the indi-
                  vidual who drove the chariot when Hector's
                  dead body was dragged through the city.
                  Male, 40, manufacturer. August 7, 1929.

**5717-5**        Hector. According to the readings, in real life
                  Hector was cruel and hated by the Trojan
                  people and was even called, "the one without
                  heart." (2886-1) His overthrow had been part
                  of a conspiracy involving both Trojans and
                  Greeks. Male, 33, printer and advertiser. No-
                  vember 7, 1923.

# Appendix C:
# References and Recommended Reading

Allen, Susan Heuck. *Finding the Walls of Troy: Frank Calvert and Heinrich Schliemann at Hisarlik*. Berkeley, California: University of California Press. 1990.

Bro, Harmon Hartzell, Ph.D. *A Seer Out of Season: the Life of Edgar Cayce*. New York: New American Library. 1989

Bulfinch, Thomas. *Bulfinch's Mythology*. New York: The Modern Library. 1998.

Cayce, Edgar (readings). Virginia Beach, Virginia: Edgar Cayce Foundation, © 1971, 1993, 1994, 1995, 1996.

Church, W.H. *The Lives of Edgar Cayce*. Virginia Beach, Virginia: A.R.E. Press. 1995.

Crawley, R. *The Complete Writings of Thucydides*. New York: The Modern Library. 1934.

Fitzgerald, Robert, translator. *The Aeneid—Virgil*. New York: Vintage Classics. 1990.

Fitzgerald, Robert, translator. *The Iliad—Homer*. New York: Anchor Books. 1989.

Fitzgerald, Robert, translator. *The Odyssey—Homer*. New York: Farrar, Straus and Giroux. 1998.

Guerber, H.A. *Myths of Greece and Rome*. New York: American Book Company. 1893.

Payne, Robert. *The Gold of Troy*. New York: Funk & Wagnall's Company. 1959.

Rieu, E.V., translator. *Homer—The Iliad*. New York: Penguin Putnam Inc. 1950.

Schliemann, Heinrich. *Ilios, the City and Country of the Trojans*. New York: Arno Press. 1976.

Way, A.S., translator. *Quintus Smyrnaeus: The Fall of Troy*. Cambridge, Massachusetts: Harvard University Press. 1913.

Wood, Michael. *In Search of the Trojan War*. Oxford, England: Facts on File. British Broadcasting Company. 1985.

# Index

# N

Neoptolcmus 54, 63, 65, 68, 126, 135, 137,
138, 142, 143
Neptune, see Poseidon 4, 57, 59, 60, 65, 69
Nestor 15, 27, 34, 35, 36, 51, 53, 114, 138

# O

Oath of Tyndareus 7, 10, 15, 115, 120
Odysseus xiii, xv, 5, 7, 11, 15, 17, 27, 34, 35,
36, 38, 47, 48, 50, 51, 52, 53, 54, 55, 56,
59, 66, 85, 112, 113, 117, 123, 125, 127,
128, 129, 131, 132, 134, 135, 136, 138,
139, 141, 143, 144, 145
*Odyssey* xiii, xiv, 48, 51, 52, 53, 54, 55, 63,
112, 113, 124, 138, 141
Œnone 6, 115, 139
Oracle of Apollo 66, 126, 139

# P

Palamedes 15, 139
Palinurus 69, 139, 142
Pallas 70, 71, 132, 139
Pandaros 30, 31, 140
Paris xii, xiv, 5, 6, 8, 9, 10, 27, 28, 29, 32, 33,
34, 42, 46, 48, 56, 60, 61, 70, 77, 78, 79,
115, 116, 119, 125, 127, 128, 133, 134,
137, 139, 140, 141, 142, 145, 147
Patroklos 36, 37, 38, 39, 41, 114, 124, 127,
133, 140
Peleus 7, 141
Penelope 7, 15, 51, 52, 55, 113
Penthesilea 43, 141
Philoctetes 47, 140, 141
Pluto, see Hades 4
Polydore 66, 141
Polyphemus, see Cyclops 51, 68
Polyxena 46, 112, 142
Poseidon 3, 4, 5, 38, 39, 51, 55, 57, 116, 138,
139, 141, 142, 143
Priam 6, 9, 42, 46, 54, 65, 84, 88, 129, 133,
138, 140, 142
Protesilaus 18, 19, 134, 136, 142
Proteus 55, 143
Pyrrhus 54, 138, 143

# Q

Quintus Smyrnaeus 63

# R

Remus 57, 71, 143
Roman Empire xiv, 56, 114, 120, 124
Romolus 57, 70, 71
Romulus 126, 143

# S

Schliemann, Ekaterina Lishin 77, 84
Schliemann, Heinrich xv, xviii, 21, 73, 74,
75, 76, 77, 78, 79, 80, 83, 84, 85
Schliemann, Sophia Engastromenos 84,
87
Shroyer, Linden xvii, 109
Sibyl 69, 70, 143
Silvius 70, 71, 125, 136, 144
Sinon 59, 63, 144
Sthenelus 63, 144

# T

Telemachus 15, 51, 52, 53, 54, 55, 114, 115,
136, 141, 144
Telephus 10, 144
Thessandrus 63, 145
Thetis 7, 8, 11, 12, 26, 41, 116, 124, 132, 136,
145
Thoas 63, 145
Thucydides 120
Trojan horse xii, xiii, xiv, xviii, 48, 49, 55,
56, 58, 59, 60, 63, 94, 116, 123, 132,
136, 137, 138, 144, 145, 149, 152
Turnus 70, 71, 139, 145
Tyndareus 6, 7, 120, 133, 137, 139, 145

# U

Ulysses, see Odysseus xiii, 56, 59, 63, 68,
70

# V

Venus, see Aphrodite 4, 57, 58, 65, 68, 69,
70
Vesta, see Hestia 4